Using The New Oxford School Dictionary

John Butterworth

Illustrations by Jocelyn Wild

(Teacher's Book)

Oxford University Press 1992

Introduction

Using The New Oxford School Dictionary is a stimulating book of exercises and games to be used alongside *The New Oxford School Dictionary*. The book has two parts:

Part one, *Using The Dictionary*, provides a basic guide to the workings of *The New Oxford School Dictionary*, and encourages its use as a source not only of information but also of pleasure and amusement.

Part two, *Exploring Language*, contains activities that broaden into a series of language themes, such as the origins of English, the way its words are formed and used, and how they change and evolve. In the process, some strong cross-curricular links are established with history, geography, technology, science, maths, and modern languages.

Using The New Oxford School Dictionary is targeted at Key Stage 3, and within this band offers a wide range of tasks and challenges. Whilst the language level, especially in Part two, is sufficiently demanding to extend the students' vocabulary and linguistic experience to the full, the activities can be approached in a great variety of ways to suit wide-ranging needs. Practically all the questions and assignments lend themselves to discussion prior to (or in place of) written answers; and many teachers will want to use the activities this way, so that students can benefit from each other's ideas, working – and playing the games – together.

Using The New Oxford School Dictionary satisfies requirements in all five attainment targets of the National Curriculum, approximately between levels 4 and 8 inclusive. Some of the statements of attainment are addressed directly in the subject matter: amongst them, AT1 6(d), AT2 5(d), AT4/5 7(a). Others are encountered less directly, as a product of the activity: contributing to a discussion (AT1), improving spelling (AT4), or turning to other reference materials to pursue an enquiry (AT2).

Contents

Part one Using the Dictionary

Dictionary Quiz	2
Entries	3
Order	4
Discussion and Group Work	5
What it Means	6
Numbered Entries	7
Words in Use	8
Word-Stairs *a game*	9
Word Classes	10
Duffinitions *a game*	12
Singular and Plural	13
Verb Forms	14
Derivatives	16
Pronunciation	17
Phrases	18
Usage	19
Connections *a game*	20
Origins	21
Appendices	22
Acrostic Definitions	23

Part two Exploring Language

Synonyms	24
What Kind / What Difference?	25
Opposites	26
Word Associations	27
Male and Female	28
Compound Words	29
Prefixes	30
Suffixes	31
Roots	32
Word Stems	34
Inflexions	35
The Origins of English	36
How Words Develop	37
Language Groups	38
Old English	40
Middle English	42
Latin	44
Greek	46
Science and Technology	47
Word Travels *a game*	48
Nouns and Pronouns	50
He, She, It or They? *a quiz*	51
Adjectives	52
Complements *a game*	54
Adverbs	55
Actions	56
Feelings	57
True or False? *a quiz*	58
What's the Connection? *a quiz*	59
New Words	60
Answers	62

Part one **Using the Dictionary**

Dictionary Quiz

What can you find out from a dictionary?
Use your *New Oxford School Dictionary* to answer the questions in the quiz.

1 What is **saffron** used for in cooking?
2 What language does the word **safari** come from?
3 What do the letters of the word **derv** stand for?
4 Whereabouts is an animal's **hock**?
5 Around what date is the winter **solstice**?
6 What does an **osteopath** do for a living?
7 Would you be wise to drink something **noxious**?
8 What colours are the flowers on a **magnolia** tree?
9 What do the two halves of the word **dinosaur** mean, and what ancient language do they come from?
10 How many players can take part in a game of **mah-jong**?
11 Where does a **Catherine wheel** get its name?
12 In the word **longevity**, how is the *g* pronounced?
   i   as in *long*   ii   as in *orange*.
13 Which word is incorrectly used in the sentence:
   'Good food will insure good health'?   What is the correct word?
14 What is the connection between the month of **September** and the number **seven**?
15 What name is given to the people of:
   i **Finland**   ii **Ghana**   iii **Cyprus**?

Discussion

Who was James Watt and what does the dictionary tell you about him?

Why do you think Watt's name is mentioned in the dictionary? Are all famous people included? If not, try to find the names of some who are included and think of some others who are left out.

Entries

Each word in the dictionary and the information given with it is called an **entry**. Here is a typical entry, with its parts labelled:

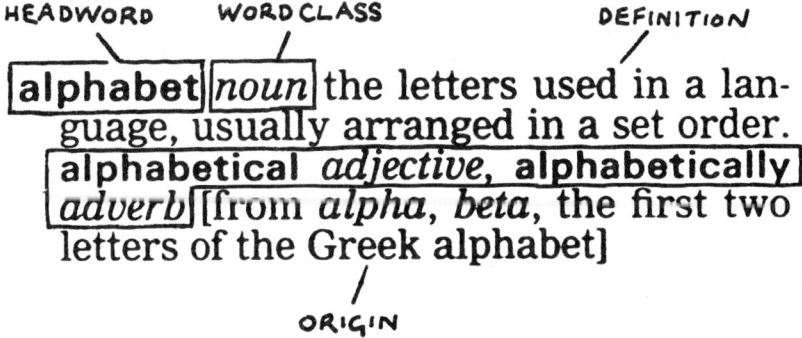

1. Which part of the entry tells you what the headword means?
   Which part of the entry tells you what sort of word the headword is?
   Which part of the entry tells you where the word came from?
   Which part of the entry lists some other words which are close to the headword in spelling and meaning, but are used in different ways?

2. Copy and label the following entries:

   concussion   **dynamic**   **tempt**

Discussion

Do all entries contain the same amount of information?
Look at, and discuss, these entries in particular:

desiccated   **onlooker**   **tubular**
graze *verb*   **helix**   **compulsory**

Order

Can you see what is special about the letters of the word **begin**? The letters are in alphabetical order:

a **b** c d **e** f g h **i** j k l m **n** o p r s t u v w x y z

1. If you rearrange the following groups of letters into alphabetical order, they will each spell an English word.

   wonk   stif   nich   thogs   potad   scocta

   Work out what the six words are then write them down in an alphabetical list.

   With the help of a dictionary, find **five** more words whose letters are in alphabetical order.

2. The headwords in a dictionary are in alphabetical order, to make them easier to find.

   Sort the following sets of words into the order in which you would find them in the dictionary.

   motion   mystery   meeting   mutiny   maximum

   pleasure   parade   punctual   predict   poetry

   slow   slender   sleepy   slippery   slack

   these   theirs   they   them   then

3. What do you notice about the order of the words in the next sentence?

   Animals cannot easily escape from the zoo.

   Can you make up any similar ones?

Discussion and Group Work

1 If you look in the Yellow Pages of the telephone directory, you will find that many businesses have names like:

ABC Taxis   Abacus Computers   Baa-baa Wool Suppliers

The idea is to be near to the top of the alphabetical list. Why, do you think?

Using the dictionary, invent a clever, catchy name for each of the following kinds of business. It should be near the beginning of the alphabet

a pet shop   a health food restaurant   a mobile disco

Working as a group, put all the names you have thought up into an alphabetical list, as they would appear in the telephone directory.

2 One of the disadvantages of an alphabetical dictionary is the difficulty in finding a word when you don't yet know how to spell it.

For example, imagine you had just heard these two words for the first time:

hygiene   hijack

How many different spellings might you try before you find them?

i Discuss, and make a list of, the most problematic letters in the English alphabet; and of some words that are difficult to find until you know the right spelling. You could test their difficulty by saying them aloud and asking other people to look them up.

ii Can you think of any other system by which words could be stored and found? What would be the advantages and disadvantages of your system?

Library Assignment

Find and list some other books, besides dictionaries, which have lots of entries in a certain order. Is the order always alphabetical?

What it Means

One of the main functions of a dictionary is to give the meanings of words. In most entries this information is provided by the part called the **definition**. For example:

lifeboat *noun* a boat for rescuing people at sea.

A definition has to be exact. It must give the full meaning of the headword.

1 Write a short definition of your own for each of the words below. Then look in the dictionary and compare its definition with yours.

mainland   obstacle   conquer   fish   seven   grey

Revise and rewrite your definition if you think it needs improvement.

2 Many words have more than one meaning. When this is so, the definitions are numbered, as they are in this entry:

judge *noun* 1 a person appointed to hear cases in a lawcourt and decide what should be done. 2 a person deciding who has won a contest or competition, or the value or quality of something.

Look up the following words and count the number of separate definitions each one has.

harsh   dry *(adjective)* **abuse** *(verb)* **explode   follow   out**

Discussion

Look up these five words:

do   go   to   after   some

How do you think they and their meanings are different from most other English words? Can you think of a few other examples to add to the list?

Numbered Entries

mail¹ *noun* letters or parcels etc. sent by post.

mail² *noun* armour made of metal rings joined together, *a suit of chain-mail.*

These are not two definitions for the same word. **mail**¹ and **mail**² are entirely different words that happen to be spelt in the same way.

Words like these are called *homographs*, and are shown by the small numbers immediately after the headword.

1. Look up **homograph** in the dictionary. What does the dictionary give as an example of a homograph? How is a *homograph* different from a *homophone*?

2. Look up the following homographs. How many different entry numbers are there for each one?

   bass   batten   bay   fell   felt   fast   sound   lay

3. Here are some words with short definitions next to them. Are they different definitions for the same word, or are the words homographs? (If they are homographs, the dictionary will give them separate, numbered entries.)

   overdo do something too much
   overdo cook food for too long

   deal a bargain or agreement
   deal a kind of wood

   hover wait about, linger
   hover hang in the air

   hind at the back
   hind a female deer

   date a certain day
   date an arrangement to meet

Words in Use

The meaning of a word is not always clear from the definition alone. It is often helpful to see how a word is used in a sentence or phrase.

In the following entry there is an example of the headword in use; it is printed in *italics*.

continual *adjective* continuing for a long time without stopping or with only short breaks, *Stop this continual quarrelling!* **continually** adverb.

1. Look up these words in the dictionary and write the example or examples that are given for them.

    definite   **makeshift**   **other** *adjective*   **virtual**   **zoom**

    Why do some entries need more than one example?

2. Here are several words, each with a definition. Try to write examples - phrases or short sentences - which make these meanings clear. Then compare your examples with the ones given in the dictionary.

    absent *adjective* not here; not present

    flow *verb* gush out

    maul *verb* injure by handling or clawing

    offend *verb* do wrong

    deluge *noun* something coming in great numbers

Word-Stairs

A game for two or more players

TABLE
   BLESSING
      INGREDIENT
         ENT...

Each stair is formed by taking the last three letters of a word and using them as the first three letters of a new word.

How far can you continue the stairs without repeating any of the words? You can use the dictionary to help you.

Make *word-stairs* into a game using sheets of squared paper, each with a *starting line* drawn five columns from the left, and a *finishing line* five lines from the right. You will need around twenty columns in between - more when you become expert.

```
PART
 ARTISTIC
     TICKLES
        LESSON
```

To begin with each player chooses a word of four or five letters and writes it behind the starting line. On the word 'go' the players construct *word-stairs* as fast as they can. The first across the finishing line is the winner.

No word may be used more than once.

Only dictionary words count; use the dictionary as the 'referee'.

Word Classes

As you have probably noticed, every headword in the dictionary is followed by one of these words in italics:

noun   pronoun   adjective   verb   adverb

preposition   conjunction   interjection   abbreviation   prefix

These are called **word classes** or **parts of speech**. They tell you what kind of word the headword is and how it can be used in a sentence.

1 Look up the following words and write down the word class each one belongs to:

old   ocean   often   operate   or   oh   OPEC

2 Which word class do these belong to?

horse   hospital   hockey   helicopter   hill

3 And these?

come   carry   calculate   choose   chew

Word classes are the name for *sets* of words. Here is a set of adjectives:

good   green   glossy   gloomy   gigantic

4 Write out a set of:

   i five *adjectives* beginning with **r**
   ii five *adverbs* beginning with **s**
   iii five *nouns* beginning with **t**

A word can belong to more than one class.

cheat verb **1** trick or deceive somebody. **2** try to do well in an examination or game etc. by breaking the rules.

cheat noun a person who cheats.

The headword appears twice in the entry, once as a verb and once as a noun.

5 Look up the following words and note how many different word classes each one belongs to.

lift   limit   little   light¹   light²

6 This is a *Venn diagram*. It shows words belonging to one, two, or three classes.

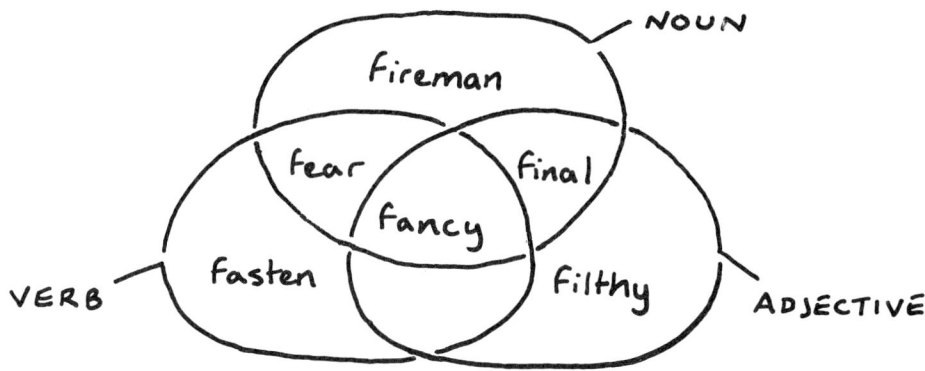

From the diagram:

  i pick out a word which can only be a *noun*
  ii pick out a word which can be a *noun* or a *verb*
  iii pick out a word which can be a *noun* or a *verb* or an *adjective*

7 Draw a Venn diagram and place these words on it correctly, after looking them up in the dictionary:

open   paint   create   cold   double   eyesight   imaginary

8 How many word classes do each of these words belong to, and which classes are they?

home   test   sound   east   run

Duffinitions
A game for two or more players

What is the correct definition of the following word?

myriad (*say* mirri-ad)

   i an adjective meaning innumerable, too many to count
  ii a noun meaning shiny metal that reflect light
 iii a verb meaning show surprise or amazement.

Two of the choices are *duffinitions*: they are completely wrong. If you don't know the word, **myriad**, have a guess at its meaning and then use the dictionary to see if you are right.

You can play *Duffinitions* between teams of three or four, but it requires some preparation.

With the help of the dictionary, each member of the team writes down a word that no one else is likely to know, along with one proper definition. The others in the team write a *duffinition* for it. Obviously, you must keep your preparations secret.

The idea of the game is to challenge the opposing team to pick the correct definition from the three or four alternatives that you read to them. If they choose the true definition, they score a point; if they don't, you score.

Singular and Plural

Nouns are words which stand for things.

Most nouns have two forms: *singular* when they stand for one thing, *plural* when they stand for two or more.

1. Sort these nouns into two sets, singular and plural:

   town   river   horses   girl   friend   shoes

   nose   cradle   engines   computer   politicians

   How can you tell the singular and plural forms apart?

   Which forms of these nouns does the dictionary give: singular, plural, or both?

2. Write down the plural forms of the following nouns:

   church   ferry   calf   wife   spy   tooth

   potato   helix   child   aircraft   formula   fish

   Which forms of these nouns does the dictionary give - singular, plural, or both - and why?

3. What is unusual about the following nouns? (See if you can work out the answer before looking the words up in the dictionary.)

   scissors   trousers   bellows   graffiti   gymnastics   data

4. Sort these words into singular and plural nouns:

   dahlia   criteria   media   fuchsia   bacteria

Discussion

If a witch's recipe said, 'add four sheep's eyes to the potion . . .' how many eyes would you add - four or eight?

If, instead, the recipe said 'add four pig's trotters . . .' how many trotters would you need?

What have these questions got to do with singular and plural nouns?

Verb Forms

Verbs come in a number of different forms.

Look up the verb **break**. It gives four forms: the headword and three in brackets.

break *verb* (**broke, broken, breaking**) 1 divide or fall into pieces ...

1. Write four short sentences, showing how the different forms of **break** can be used.

   Which of your sentences are in the *past tense* (about something that has happened at an earlier time)?

2. The usual, or *regular*, way to form the past tense of a verb is to add the letters **-ed**.

   happen > happened

   Look up **happen**. Its **-ed** and **-ing** forms are not spelt out because they are regular: they follow the rules exactly.

   Write the **-ed** and **-ing** forms of these regular verbs:

   call   stay   work   express   intend

3. The following verbs are also regular, but adding **-ed** or **-ing** causes slight changes to the spelling. Write the **-ed** and **-ing** forms, and then check them in the dictionary.

   explode   stop   plan   cry   compel

4. These next verbs are *irregular*: they have different rules. Write down their past tense and **-ing** forms and then check them in the dictionary.

   come   run   weep   sleep   fight

5. Do the same with these, which are a mixture of regular and irregular verbs.

   benefit   bring   commit   limit   manage

   Which are the regular ones?

As well as an ordinary past tense, some verbs have a special form for use in sentences like this one:

    She has **broken** her promise.

It is called the *past participle*.

1 Use the dictionary to find out the past tense and the past participle of these verbs:

eat   wake   write   speak   do

2 Take the ten verb forms you collected in question one and write an example of the way each one is used. The example should be a short but complete sentence. Examples:

    Who broke this window?
    You have broken your promise.

3 The **-ing** form of a verb is called the *present participle*. Write five short sentences containing the present participles of each of these verbs:

flap   ski   reply   shine   damage

4 Try looking up the verb **grew** in the dictionary. You won't find it unless you look under **grow**.

Under which headword must you look to find the following verbs?

thought   challenged   won   smiling   risen

Derive
Derivatives

A derivative is a word which comes from another word, usually with some small change to its spelling or pronunciation. For example:

conjure *verb* (**conjured, conjuring**) perform puzzling tricks
    conjuror *noun*

Conjuror is a *derivative* of **conjure**.

Also look up **report** and **reporter**.

1. Write two sentences, one giving an example of how the verb **conjure** (or **conjured**) is used and the other giving an example of how the noun **conjuror** is used. Do the same for **report** and **reporter**.

2. What do you call someone who does each of the following?

    cycles   instructs   invents   grumbles   grovels   competes

    corresponds   represents   applies (for a job)   **enters** (a race)

3. The word in brackets does not fit the following sentence, but one of its derivatives does. Which one?

    Tomorrow is expected to start [**fog**].

    The answer, of course, is **foggy**.

    i. Which derivative of the word in brackets is needed to correct each of the following sentences?

    The weather did not spoil the [**magnificent**] of the occasion.
    Many children were [**orphan**] by the earthquake.
    That is [**total**] the wrong [**explain**].
    The expedition came [**perilous**] close to disaster.
    The event was of great [**history**] [**important**].
    There has been a sharp [**intensify**] of [**hostile**].
    New members have to attend an [**initiate**] ceremony.

    ii. Make a table showing the word class of each of the words in brackets and the word class of the derivative you replaced it with. Example:

    fog *noun* > **foggy** *adjective*

Pronunciation

The work on this page needs to be done in pairs or small groups.

Before starting, read and discuss the notes about pronunciation in the front of the dictionary.

1. Taking turns, say each of the following words aloud, whilst your partner checks in the dictionary that you have pronounced it correctly.

   You may well have to look at the list of sounds on page xii as well as the entry itself.

   fuselage   **connive**   **house** *verb*   **grotesque**   **bass**[1]

   depleted   **excerpt**   **intrigue**   **hectare**   **maelstrom**

   prestige   **hypothesis**   **vociferous**   **fluorescent**   **sceptic**

   prologue   **viscous**   **ricochet**   **visage**   **sedentary**

2. Words can be divided into *syllables*, i.e. single sounds. How many syllables has each of the following words?

   cough   **initiative**   **jeopardy**   **courier**   **indubitable**

3. Part of the correct pronunciation is putting *stress* on the right syllable. Re-read the note on page xii in the dictionary and then say which syllable in the following words is spoken with the most stress. Example:

   chaos is pronounced **kay**-oss, with the stress on the first of its two syllables.

   ionosphere   **medieval**   **inexorable**   **progress** *verb*

   progress *noun*

4. Repeat, aloud, all the words you have met on this page. Then try to put each one into a spoken sentence which shows how it can be used.

Phrases

The word **hang** generally means to support something from above. But what is meant by the phrases:

hang about   hang back   hang on   hang up?

Phrases like these are called *idioms*. They have their own special meanings.

1 What is meant by the following idioms?
The headwords where you will find the idioms are in italics.

make **off** with the money
on the *move* again
get **your own back** on someone
come **by** a large sum of money
talking **behind** a person's back
back **out** of an agreement
play **down** a crisis
take a joke **in good** *part*
appear **in** *person*
be **on** *hand* in case of emergency

2 Many of the idioms given in the dictionary are marked by the word *(informal)*. What do you think this means? (You will find the answer on page ix at the front of the dictionary.)

3 Write down six idioms that you use frequently. Look to see if they are in the dictionary.

Usage

19

Be careful how you use some words.

Where a word is frequently used wrongly, or where there is a confusing similarity between two words, the dictionary warns you. For example:

curb *verb* restrain.
curb *noun* a restraint, *Put a curb on spending.* USAGE Do not confuse with *kerb*.

1 Look at the following pairs of sentences. In each case, say which sentence is correct.

    a You must learn to curb your impatience.
    b Don't step off the curb if there is traffic coming.

    c There are two alternate styles to choose from.
    d The strange craft was glowing in alternate colours.

    e Being in Scotland at the time of the murder gave me an alibi.
    f Saying that it was only an accident is no alibi.

    g There was no mistaking her distinct way of dressing.
    h This time the sound was quite distinct.

    i There have been tales of strange phenomena at the house.
    j Ghosts are one phenomena I can't bring myself to take seriously.

    k The hotel accommodation was really luxuriant.
    l Part of his disguise was a luxuriant black beard.

    m My grandmother is a compulsive supporter of Liverpool F.C.
    n It is compulsive to wear crash-helmets on site.

    o It's no good trying to burn that: it's inflammable.
    p Inflammable gases are a danger in coal mines.

2 Can you see a way of putting right each of the incorrect sentences above, without altering more than one word in each?

Connections

A game for two or more players

Start with any word chosen for you by your opponent. It has to be a word all the players know, for example:

build

The object is to guess a word which will be used in the dictionary definition of **build**, for example:

make

Look it up. If you are right, score a point and continue. If you are wrong, that is the end of your turn. As it happens, you are right:

build *verb* make something by putting parts together ...

So now try to guess a word which will appear in the definition for **make**. For example, you might say:

cause

Right again!

make *verb* ... 3 cause or compel.

Continue your turn, or 'break', until you get one wrong. This break, for instance, could continue:

cause > **happen** > **occur** > **be** > **exist** > **alive** ...

The winner is the player who scores the longest break.

Rules

You are not allowed to use the same word more than once in a break. You are not allowed to use the words:

is   are   the   a   an   and   or   to   from

You can disregard common endings of words, such as **-ed**, **-ing**, or **s**.

For example, look up **ivory**: if you had guessed *elephant* instead of *elephants'*, it would count as being right.

Origins

English is a mixture of many languages. You can tell this by looking up the following words in the dictionary:

denim finish sugar melody billycan

bride butler potato kiosk mammoth

1. From which languages have the twelve words above come into Modern English?

2. What do the origins of the following words have in common?

   dahlia braille welly cardigan sandwich joule

3. The words in the next group have curious origins. Try to guess where they come from before looking them up.

   deadline juggernaut lord truncheon laser harass

   thug robot tulip tadpole poll tax dodo

4. These words have the same origin:

What is the origin? Copy the diagram and write the origin in the circle.

Draw similar diagrams showing the shared origins of these pairs or groups of words:

liberate liberty

mortify mortal

battle battery batter

vengeance vindictive vendetta

sign signal signature signet

Appendices Append

Look up **January** and **Monday**. Whereabouts in the dictionary are these words to be found? (The *Contents* page at the front will help you.)

Now answer these questions:

1. What is a *prefix*? Underline the prefix in each of the following words:

   hexagon   omnivorous   distraction   universe   periscope

2. What is a *suffix*? Underline the suffix in each of these words:

   democracy   highest   clockwise   musician   telepathy

3. From which language have each of these expressions been borrowed? What do they mean in English?

   ad nauseam   doppelgänger   laissez-faire   hara-kiri

   sotto voce   eureka   faux pas   bona fide

4. From which language have the English names for the days of the week come down, and what are they all named after?

5. From which language have the English names for the months of the year come down?

6. What is the difference between an American pint and a British pint?

7. If the weather forecast tells you it is going to be eighty-six degrees Fahrenheit in the shade, what temperature can you expect on the Celsius scale?

Acrostic Definitions

Look up the word **acrostic**. What does it mean?

Here is an example of an acrostic in which each line is a definition, or part of a definition, of the word spelt by the initial letters:

Sun
Twinkling point of light in the night sky
A shape with several pointed arms
Really famous performer

The word is **STAR**.

1. If you rearrange these definitions, you can make an acrostic like the one in the example above. What is the word it spells?

   Exert pressure
   Verb used informally to mean 'throw'
   Action of lifting something heavy
   Hard push
   Expend a lot of effort

2. Here there are *two* sets of definitions, or parts of definitions, mixed together. Can you sort them out into two separate *acrostic* definitions? What are the two words they spell?

   Adjective meaning weak
   Cul-de-sac, dead end
   Even, well-matched
   Faded
   Nearly unconscious
   Local
   Indistinct
   The opposite of clear
   Of things that are near by
   Stuffy

3. Try to make up one or two acrostic definitions of your own. Then mix them up and try them on someone else.

Part two **Exploring language**

Synonyms = Synonyms

The king had all his enemies thrown in **gaol**.
The king had all his enemies thrown in **prison**.

These two sentences mean the same, because **gaol** and **prison** are *synonyms*.

1. Find a synonym for each of the words in bold in the following sentences:

   You must **obtain** permission before you can camp here.
   What she said did not make a very **cogent** argument.
   Every **individual** vote has to be counted.
   I don't think you **appreciate** the **magnitude** of the problem.
   Some of the gang were **apprehended** at the airport.
   The members of the expedition planned their **itinerary meticulously**.
   This unexpected development **scuppered** our plans.
   The **odour** of stale tobacco smoke **permeated** the room.

2. Make up short sentences in which the following pairs of words mean the same. Follow the example for **gaol** and **prison** at the top of the page.

   abortive; unsuccessful   **variable; changeable**

   film; layer   **indirect; circuitous**   **flooded; inundated**

   tools; implements   **empty; void**   **tarnish; blemish**

3. Do you think there are any pairs of words that are always synonyms, whatever sentences they are used in? Experiment with the following words, and try to think up some examples of your own.

   die; perish   **slope; incline**   **freedom; liberty**

   incredible; unbelievable   **follow; pursue**

   What conclusion have you come to?

4. Why do you think there are so many English words with roughly the same meaning as the noun **smell**? For example:

   odour   aroma   stink   stench   whiff   pong   scent

   Are there certain occasions when you would use one word but not the others; and, if so, why?

What Kind?
What Difference?

falcon *noun* a kind of hawk often used in the sport of hunting other birds or game. **falconry** *noun*

1. What kind of bird is a falcon?
   What makes a falcon different from other birds of the same kind?

   A useful way to define something is to say what it is like (its *kind*), and then what makes it special (its *difference*). For example:

WORD	KIND	DIFFERENCE
mayfly	insect	lives for a short time, in spring

2. What kinds and what differences does the dictionary give in its definitions of these words? Continue the table.

   hangar   mead   crocus   gondola   thirteen

3. The word for a kind is often called a *general term*. **Hawk** is a more general term than **falcon**; but **bird** is a more general term than **hawk**.

   With the help of the dictionary, put the following words into their order of generality, with the most general term first.

   fungus, mushroom, plant   snail, animal, gastropod

   communication, gossip, talk   offal, liver, sustenance

   mineral, matter, zinc, metal   biology, study, science, botany

4. Write your own short defintions for the following, saying what kind of thing each one is and what makes it different:

   skyscraper   submarine   constable   dictionary   moon

Opposites | Opposites

absent *adjective* not here; not present,
absent from school. **absence** *noun*

present and **absent** are *opposite* in meaning.

1. Write one word which is opposite in meaning to each of the following:

   far   fiction   concave   humble   stingy

2. Opposites are often formed by adding **un-** or **in-** to the beginning of a word. For example:

   exciting > unexciting

   Produce the opposites of the following adjectives in the same way:

   usual   frequent   expensive   prejudiced   sane

3. For each of the words you produced in the last exercise, find another word or short phrase which means the same. For example:

   unexciting = dull

4. What does each of these words mean, and what is its opposite?

   anticlimax   nonsense   irrelevant   immobile   posterior

5. What is the opposite of:
   i   the **maximum** daytime temperature?
   ii   a **deciduous** tree?
   iii someone who is an **extrovert**?
   iv   **deducting** an amount?
   v   **dissent**?
   vi   a **regular** verb?
   vii a **descending** order?

Word Associations

27

Make a copy of this page; then make five chains of words which are associated in meaning. Use a different colour for each group.

Each chain ends in one of the boxes at the bottom of the page. In the box write one word which sums up what all the words in that chain are about.

One chain has been started and finished for you.

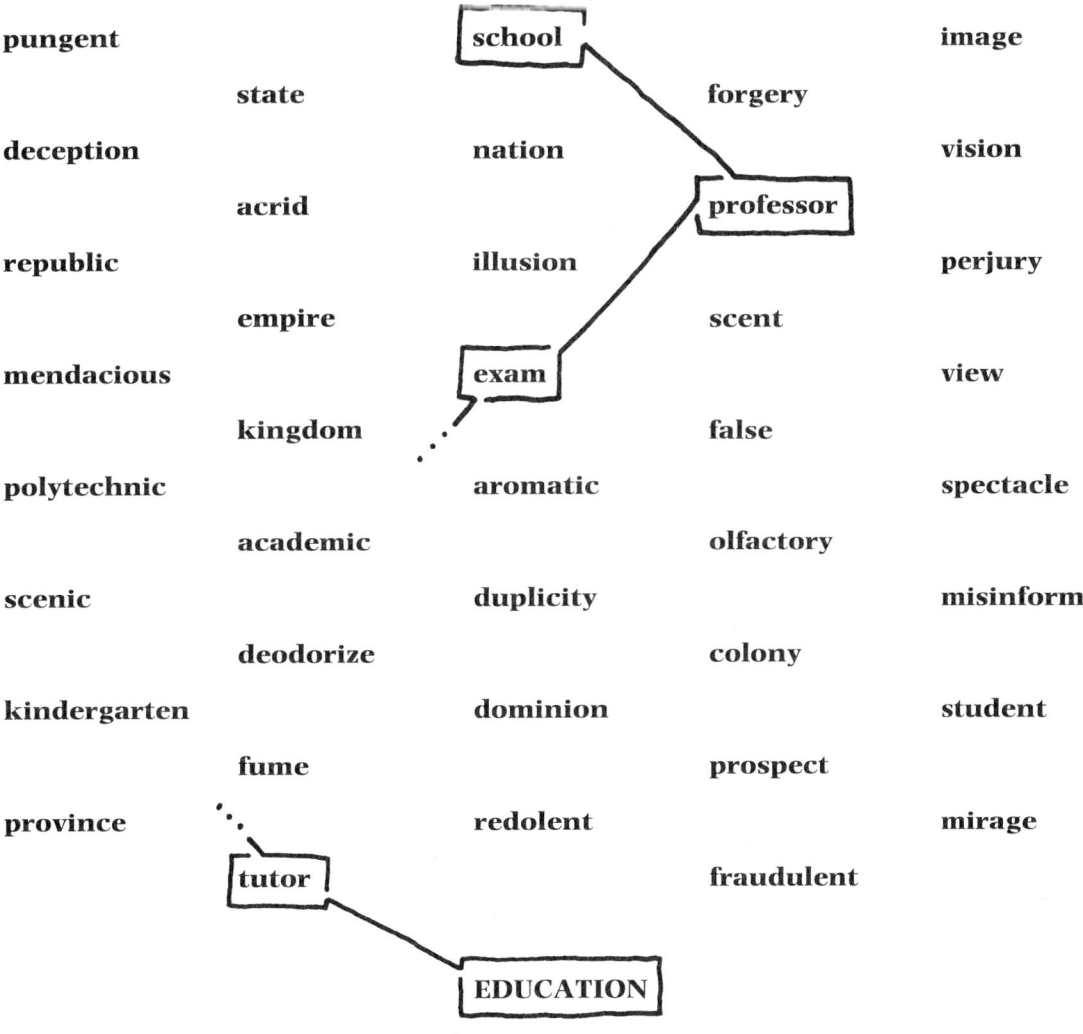

Male and Female

Many English words have a male and a female form. For example:

actor, actress   husband, wife

1 Put the following words into their correct male and female pairs:

dog   count   pen   maternal   drone   countess

vixen   feminine   cob   sire   paternal   masculine

bitch   niece   fox   queen   nephew   dam

2 What is the male equivalent of each of these words?

stewardess   heroine   manageress   sisterly   horsewoman

fiancée   femininity   Dame   bride

3 Which pairs of words, one male and one female, is covered by each of these nouns? For example, **child** covers **boy** and **girl**.

fowl   sibling   monarch   parent   foal

Discussion

Many English words end or begin with man. For instance:

spokesman   chairman   henchman   foreman

manpower   manslaughter   mankind

In which of these words should **woman** or **person** sometimes, or always, be used instead?

Think of some other, similar examples.

An **actress**, or a **waitress** has to be female, but a **doctor**, a **mechanic** or a **surveyor** can be male or female. Put together a list of occupations: how many have separate male and female titles?

You could have a class or group debate on the complaint that:

The English Language is sexist and needs to be changed!

Compound Words

1. Look up **compound**[1] in the dictionary and write down what you think a compound word is.

2. The opposite of **compound** is **simple**. Which of the following are simple words and which are compound words?

   water   fall   waterfall   breakwater   break

3. Find five more compound words and write them down together with the simple words that form them. For example:

   lifetime = life + time

4. Some compound words are *hyphenated*, i.e. the simple words that form them are joined by a dash called a *hyphen*.

   Write down the compound words which are formed from the following pairs of words, showing which ones require a hyphen and which ones do not.

   life + jacket   light + house   main + land

   sand + paper   set + up   nanny + goat

   frame + work   lift + off   pick + pocket

5. **banknote**
       notepaper
           paperback
               background
                   ground ...

   Can you make this *word-stair* longer?

   Make up some *word-stairs* of your own, using compound words.

6. The words **out** and **look** can be used to form *two* compound words,

   outlook   look-out

   Can you think of any other pairs or words which do this? (There is one example in question four.)

Prefixes

A *prefix* is an attachment to the beginning of a word. It has a meaning, but it is not a complete word. For example:

inter- *prefix* between; among. [from Latin]

1. Look up **inter-** in the dictionary and make a rough count of the number of words that begin with this prefix.

2. If you remove the prefix **inter-** from the beginning of the word **international**, you are left with another, shorter word. What is it?

   Do the same with the following words:

   interchange   interplanetary   interview   interdependent

3. Say what each of the following prefixes means and give two examples of its use in forming words:

   multi-   mono-   equi-   semi-   poly-

   Can you see what these five prefixes have in common?

4. Look up the entry for **sub-** *prefix*.
   i   What are the two meanings of **sub-**?
   ii In how many different ways can this prefix be spelt? Give an example of each one.

5. Copy and finish filling in the grid below

	pre-	**re-**	**ex-**	**anti-**
t	pretend	retire		
a	prearrange			anti-aircraft
f				
s				
v				

   Make up a similar grid with other letters and prefixes. You could invent a game using the grid, and play it within your group.

Suffixes

Look at the list of *suffixes* on pages 456-458 in the dictionary. What is the difference between a *prefix* and a *suffix*?

1. The suffix **-less** means 'without'. The example given in the dictionary is **colourless**, i.e. without colour.

   Make up a short sentence to show what each of these words means:

   hopeless   merciless   countless   ageless   useless   mindless

2. The opposite of **colourless** is **colourful**. How many other words from question one have opposites ending with the suffix **-ful**?

   Do any of the following have opposites ending with **-less**?

   awful   resentful   playful   thoughtful   handful   harmful

3. Often the spelling of a word has to be altered before a certain suffix can be added. For example:

   mercy + -less > merciless

   Copy out and complete the following:

   lazy + -est > ...

   explode + -ive > ...

   intend + -ion > ...

   pure + -ification > ...

   telephone + -ist > ...

4. The word *affix* can be used to mean any addition to a word, whether it is a prefix or a suffix. What shorter words are you left with if you strip the affixes from the following?

   plantation   premeditation   unofficially

   immortalize   consolidate   postscript

Roots Roots Roots Roots Roots Roots

Many English words can be seen to grow from the same *root*. The root **STRUCT**, for example, can be used in the formation of **construct, construction, structure** and others.

1. How many words can you build from this 'kit'?

   im-   de-   com-   sup-   ex-

   PRESS

   -ive   -ure   -ion

2. Copy the table below; then form ten words and link them to their meanings by drawing connecting lines. One is done for you.

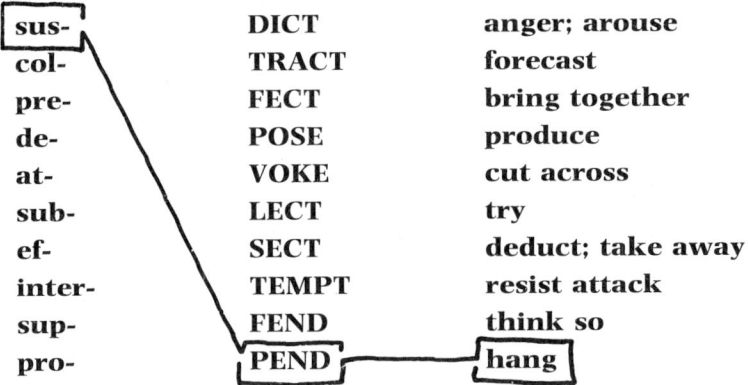

3. One root completes all the words in each row. Select the right ones from the list at the end.

   cor ... ion   dis ... ive   ... ure   inter ...

   im ...   ex ...   ... er   sup ... er   ... able   re ... er

   pre ... ence   con ... ence   inter ... ence

   FER   PENT   SENT   RUPT   PORT   RECT

In many words the spelling and pronunciation of the root are affected by the ending that follows it. For example:

describe > **descriptive**   **delude** > **delusion**

1 What nouns ending in **-ion** are formed from the following verbs?

produce   proceed   extend   expel   invade   receive   admit

2 What adjectives ending **-ive** are formed from these verbs?

exclude   destroy   explode   defend   exceed   deceive

3 i Look up the word tractor. What nearby word has the same origin?

ii Tractor is formed from the root **TRACT** which means pull or drag. Which word, from the root **TRACT**, fits each one of the spaces below?

When a cat pulls *back* its claws, it … them.
When a magnet draws something *towards* it, it … it.
When a dentist *pulls* a tooth out, she … it.

iii Write a phrase or short sentence containing each of these words:

protracted   contract   traction   detracts   intractable

4 i Look up **torsion**. What does it mean?

ii What word with the same root means each of the following?

A person who twists money out of someone by force or threats.
A person who twists his or her body into unusual shapes.
A person who deliberately causes pain or suffering to someone.

Word Stems

The *stem* is the main part of a word. By adding different endings to it you can form different words which are connected in meaning. For example:

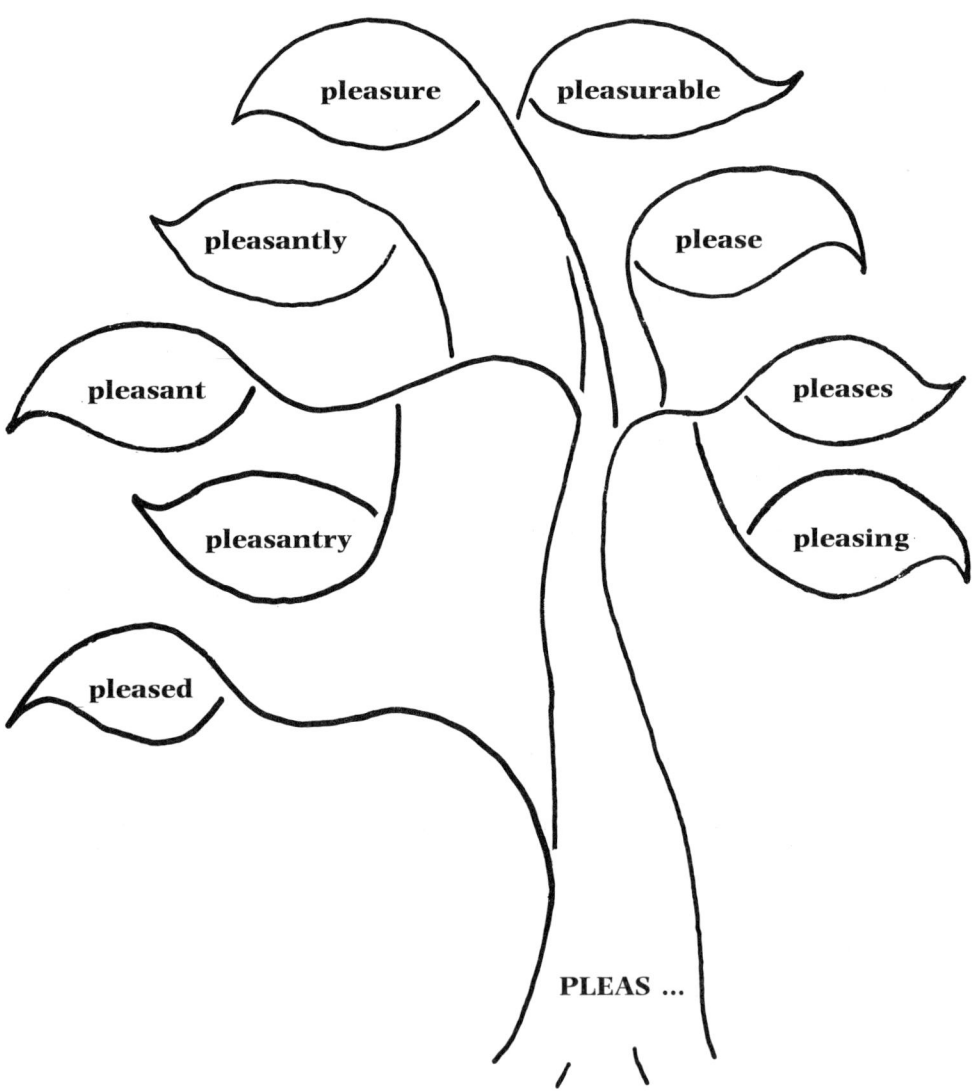

1. Construct a similar tree diagram with the stem **MANAG ...** ; and another with a word stem of your own choice.

Inflect
Inflexions

Look at the entry for **inflect**, and **read** and discuss the note on *Inflexions* and *Plurals* on pages x-xi in the dictionary.

1. Write down the correct inflexions of the verb **see** in the following examples. Each one should be different.

   I don't want to ... you here again.
   She suddenly ... something out of the corner of her eye.
   We haven't ... him around here recently.
   I'll be ... you.
   I honestly don't know what she ... in him.

2. The most inflected verb in English is **be**. How many different forms does the dictionary give, and what are they?

3. Look up the words **them** and **us** in the dictionary. When are they used instead of the forms **they** and **we**? Give examples.

4. **We** and **they** belong to the class *pronoun*. Some other pronouns also have inflexions:

   I, me   she, her   he, him

   Discuss the way the pronouns have been used in these sentences. Are any of them not Standard English; and, if not, why not?

   Me and him are good mates.
   Him and her ought to stop arguing all the time.
   Jasbir and I want to swap jobs.
   The money belongs to Stephen and I.
   Colin and me won the doubles championship.

5. Write down the plural forms of

   this woman   that man

Research

As European languages go, English has very few inflexions. In your next foreign language lesson, find out how many forms there are for the verb meaning 'see' in French or Spanish or German.

The Origins of English

England's position on the edge of Europe, and its stormy history, have meant that the English language has undergone many changes.

Before discussing and answering the questions below, read pages vi and vii in the section entitled *The English Language*, at the front of the dictionary. Also look at the map and time-chart.

1 What language would have been spoken in Britain, do you think, if there had been no invasions or conquests in the last two thousand years?

2 Who were the three main invaders to land in Britain between the fifth and eleventh centuries? Which languages did they bring with them?

3 What is the origin of the word **English**?

4 Make four short lists of English words or names which have:

  i Celtic origins
  ii Anglo-Saxon origins
  iii Norse origins
  iv Norman French origins

Discussion

It is sometimes claimed that a person speaking Welsh and a person speaking Breton (the language of Brittany in north-west France) can understand each other. If this is true, why do you think it is so?

Research

Can you name a ruler in Britain who was:

  i Celtic?
  ii Anglo-Saxon?
  iii Danish?
  iv French?

Develop
How Words Develop

1. The Latin word *manus* meant 'hand'. From it originate several English words to do with hands, or doing or making things by hand. For example:

   manufacture

   Can you find any other words which share the same origin? Write them down, with their meanings alongside.

2. Look up:

   manufacture   benefactor   artefact   fact   factory   facsimile

   What is the connection between all these words, and what does each one mean?

3. What are the following?

   polygon   hexagon   pentagon   octagon

   From which language do they all originate?

4. Look up:

   algebra   geometry   arithmetic

   Which is the odd one out, and why?

5. Guess the origins of these words and then look them up:

   alligator   bonfire   budget   derrick   meteor

   malaria   mayday   mousse   nausea   racket

6. Can you see what has happened in the development of these words?

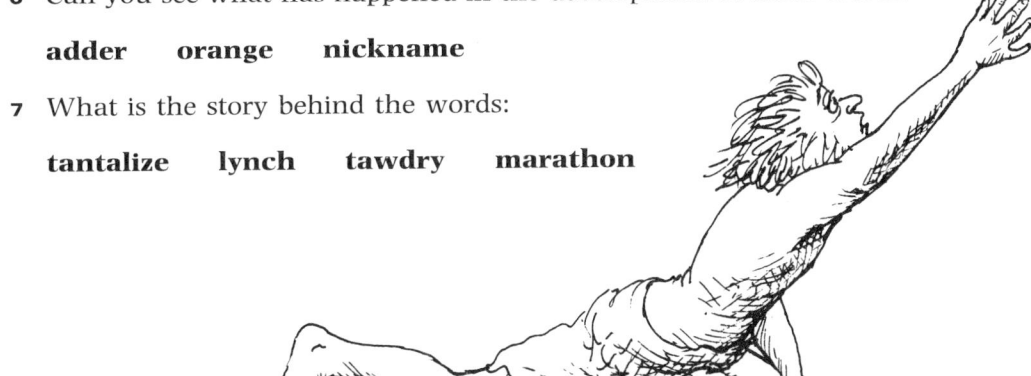

   adder   orange   nickname

7. What is the story behind the words:

   tantalize   lynch   tawdry   marathon

Language Groups

The languages of the world can be put into groups that have some similarities and shared history.

English belongs to the *Germanic* group of languages. Others in this group are German, Dutch, Flemish, and the Scandinavian languages, such as Danish.

Another closely related group of languages consists of those that developed from Latin. They are called *Romance* languages, and include French, Italian, Portuguese, and Spanish.

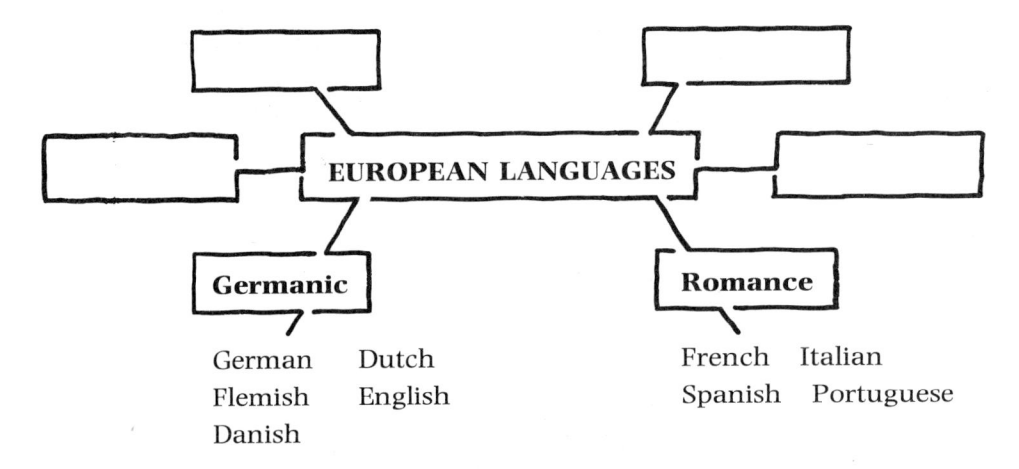

EUROPEAN LANGUAGES

Germanic

German   Dutch
Flemish English
Danish

Romance

French   Italian
Spanish Portuguese

1. Trace or copy the outline map of western Europe on the opposite page. With the help of an atlas indicate the countries where the following languages are spoken. Colour-code them: one colour for Germanic languages and another for Romance.

   Dutch   English   Flemish   French
   German   Italian   Portuguese Spanish   Danish

2. The dotted line marks the northern and western limits of the Roman Empire. Shade in the area which the Romans occupied.

   Why do you think that French, Italian, and Spanish, etc. are called Romance languages?

3. Compare your map with the map and time-chart on page vii in the dictionary. Why do you think English is called a Germanic language and not a Romance language?

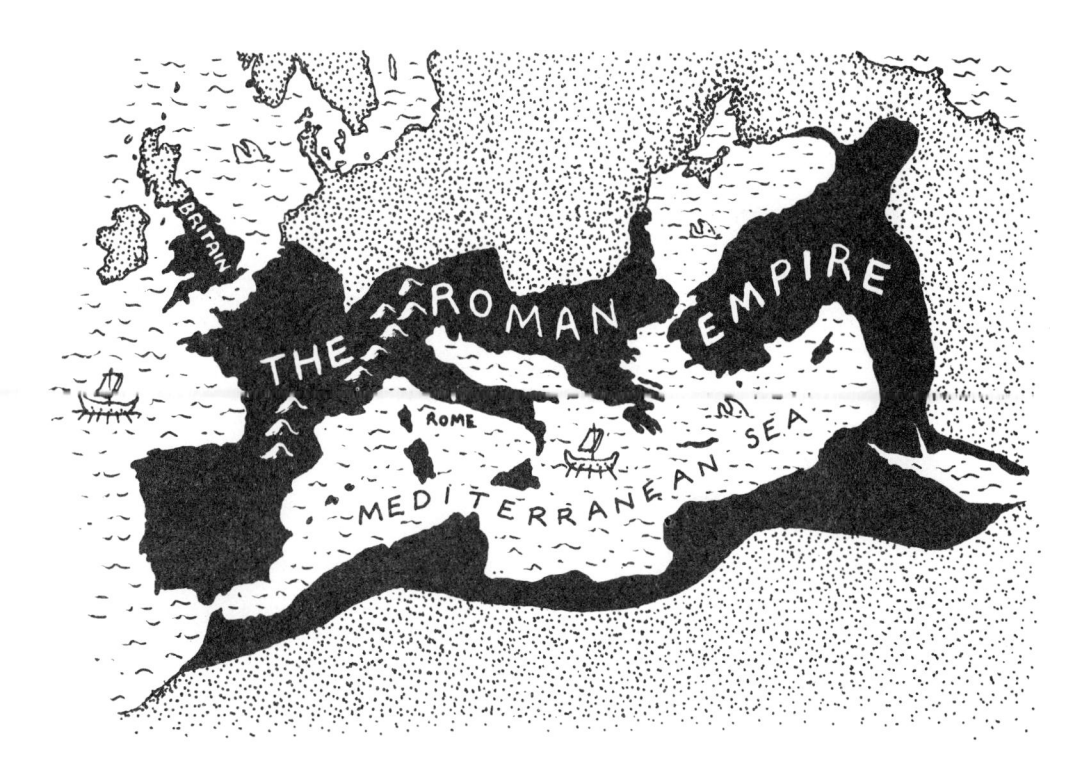

Discussion and Research

Why do you think the diagram on page 38 has some empty boxes? What belongs in them?

Find out some more about European language groups. Then copy or redesign the diagram so that you can add your new information to it.

Old English

Old English is the language that was spoken by the Angles and Saxons who invaded Britain and settled there from around AD 450.

Discussion

On the opposite page is a short piece of Old English, and below it is an approximate translation into Modern English.

How many words and phrases can you recognize in the passage as being similar to the English of today?

Apart from the words themselves, do you notice any other major differences between Old English and Modern English?

Why do you think the translation is only approximate?

1 Find out from the dictionary how these words were spelt in Old English

father   mother   brother   husband   bride

2 i What were the original meanings of the words **lord** and **lady** and how have these words changed in meaning since Anglo-Saxon times?

ii The words **well**[1] and **well**[2] are *homographs* (see page 7). So are **barrow**[1] and **barrow**[2]. Were the pairs of Old English words that they came from also homographs, or were they spelt differently?

iii The Modern English word **barn** comes from two Old English words compressed into one. What were the two words and what did they mean?

Research

serpent   snake

What are the origins of these two words, and how do they help to explain why English often has two or more names for the same thing?

With the help of a larger dictionary, or other reference books, see if you can find some more examples of duplicated words, like serpent and snake.

Ond þy ylcan gere worhte se foresprecena here geweorc be Lygan, xx mila bufan Lundenbyrig. Þa þaes on sumera foron micel dael þara burgwara, ond eac swa oþres folces, þaet hie gedydon aet þara Deniscana geweorce, ond þaer wurdon gefliemde, ond sume feower cyninges þegnas ofslaegene. Þa þaes on haerfeste þa wicode se cyng on neaweste þaere byrig, þa hwile þe hie hira corn gerypon, þaet þa Deniscan him ne mehton þaes ripes forwiernan. Þa sume daege rad se cyng up bi þaere eae, ond gehawade hwaer mon mehte þa ea forwyrcan, þaet hie ne mehton þa scipu ut brengan. Ond hie ða swa dydon: worhton ða tu geweorc on twa healfe þaere eas.

Part of the account of King Alfred's wars with the Danes from The Anglo-Saxon Chronicle, AD 896.

(The symbols **ð** and **þ** are both pronounced like **th**; the symbol **ae** is usually pronounced like the **a** in **sat**; and **sc** is pronounced like the **sh** in **she**.)

In the same year the aforementioned army built a fort by the Lea, twenty miles above London. Then later in the summer a large part of the population, and other forces as well, came to the Danish fort, and were put to flight and some four of the king's thanes (noblemen) were killed. Then the next autumn the king camped in the neighbourhood of the fort while the corn was reaped so that the Danes could not prevent the harvest. Then one day the king rode up by the river and looked to see where the river might be blocked so that they could not bring out the ships. And they did so: built two forts on the two sides of the river.

Middle English

Re-read the section on *Middle English* on pages vii-viii in the dictionary.

1 For a long time after the Norman Conquest in 1066, there were two languages spoken in England. What were they and who were they spoken by?

2 List six new words which came into use in England after the Norman Conquest.

Look at the piece of poetry on the opposite page. It was written towards the end of the fourteenth century. We call the stage the language had reached by then, Middle English.

Discussion

What main differences can you detect between the Old English passage on page 41 and this piece of Middle English?

What proportion of the words and phrases in the extract are easily recognizable?

What differences do you notice between this passage and Modern English?

The Knight's Tale

Whilom, as olde stories tellen us,
Ther was a duc that highte Theseus;
Of Atthenes he was lord and governour,
And in his tyme swich a conquerour,
That gretter was ther noon under the sonne.
Ful many a rich contree hadde he wonne;
What with his wysdom and his chivalrie,
He conquered al the regne of Femenye,
That whilom was ycleped Scithia,
And weddede the queene Ypolita,
And broughte hire hoom with hym in his contree
With muchel glorie and greet solempnytee,
And eek hir yonge suster Emylye.
And thus with victorie and with melodye
Lete I this noble duc to Atthenes ryde,
And al his hoost in armes hym besyde.

From The Canterbury Tales, by Geoffrey Chaucer

Latin

ium um
us is ius

Latin was the language of the Romans, who, for centuries, occupied large parts of Europe, including Britain.

1. With the help of the notes on Middle English in the dictionary, answer the following questions.

    i Describe three different ways in which Latin words may have found their way into the English language.

    ii English has many more Latin words in it now than it had in the ninth century. Why do you think this is?

    iii How did the words, **mint**, **pound**, **sack** and **street** find their way into English?

2. Some Latin words have become English words without any change to the spelling, although their meanings and pronunciation may have altered. Look up the following and give their English and Latin meanings.

    interim   posterior   minimum   omnibus   extra

3. Some Latin nouns have even kept their original plural forms. What are the plurals of these words, and what do they mean? (Write the answers and say the words aloud to a partner.)

    formula   curriculum   opus   genus   fungus

4. **plus** and **minus** are words we use every day in mathematics. What did they mean in Latin?

5. What did the following words mean in Latin and what do they mean now?

    ego   exit   ludo   circus   campus   video

6. The Romans gave us the word **mile**. How was a mile originally measured?

Many of the prefixes that begin English words have been borrowed from Latin.

1. i The Latin word for *round* was 'circum'. How many words can you find in the dictionary which have **circum-** as a prefix?

   ii What English words could mean the following?

   sail completely *round* something: an island or the world, for instance;
   draw a line *round* something;
   avoid something, possibly by going *round* it;
   the distance a*round* the outside of something;
   the facts sur*round*ing some event or happening.

2. Many groups of English words have Latin roots. The root **-rect-**, for example, comes from the Latin word 'rectus', meaning straight or right.

   Can you think of six more English words which share this origin?

3. **progress   aggression   congress   regression**

   What does each of these words mean?
   What has each of the words got to do with 'going'?
   Of the four words, pick two that are *opposite* in meaning.

Greek

Look at the paragraph on Greek on page viii in the dictionary.

1. When was the period of history known as the *Renaissance*, and why did so many Greek words come into the English language at that time?

2. Explain the meaning of the word **atmosphere**. How has it got its meaning from Greek words?

3. **comedy   tragedy   theatre**

   What do these three words mean, and what were their original Greek meanings?

4. Find, from the Appendix in the dictionary, what the suffix **-graphy** means, and what it meant in Greek.

   Give some examples of words which have this ending.

5. List five words which end in **-logy**. What did this suffix mean in Greek?

6. How many words can you find that begin with the letters **phys-**? What did *physis* and *physikos* mean in Greek?

7. What do the following words have in common, and which Greek word or words does each one originate from?

   autopsy   anaesthetic   physiotherapy   antibiotic   pathology

   Can you add three words which could belong to the list and which also have Greek origins? Think of words to do with medicine.

Science and Technology = mc² 47

lift-off *noun* the vertical take-off of a rocket or spacecraft.

1. The American space programme during the last thirty years has given the language many new words and expressions - or new meanings for existing words. What do the following mean?

    module   capsule   astronaut   shuttle

2. What new science do these expressions belong to, and what do they mean?

    software   hardware   byte   VDU   floppy disk

3. The following new sports have resulted from modern technology:

    windsurfing   hang-gliding   skateboarding

    Write a dictionary-style entry of your own for each of these words; then compare it with the one in The New Oxford School Dictionary.

4. What are:

    acid rain   plutonium   ozone layer   asbestos   radioactivity?

5. What are:

    nylon   polymers   polystyrene   vinyl   melamine?

6. What do the following have in common?

    watts   amps   joules   hertz   Celsius

7. What are the origins of the words:

    science   technology   physics   chemistry   atomic   zoology?

Word Travels

A game for two or more players

The English language has travelled all over the world. On its travels it has absorbed many words from other countries.

The object of this game is to circumnavigate the globe, with the help of words. You will need two counters.

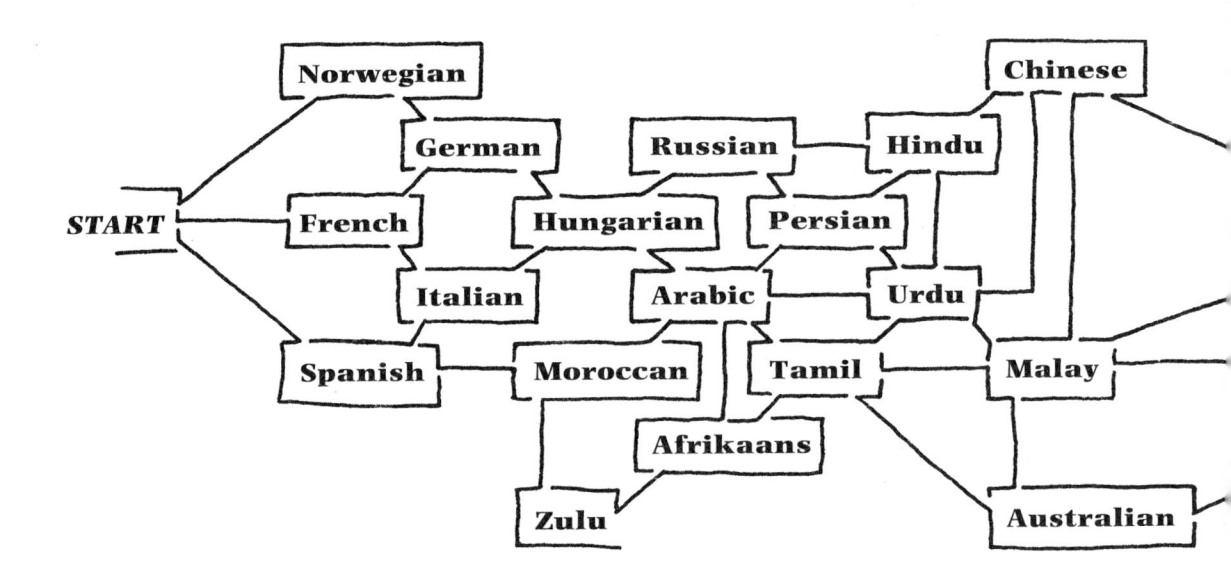

```
                    Norwegian                        Chinese
                          German     Russian    Hindu
START      French            Hungarian    Persian
                 Italian          Arabic        Urdu
           Spanish       Moroccan       Tamil       Malay
                              Afrikaans
                       Zulu                      Australian
```

amok   battalion   cherish   magazine   pyjamas
barracks   orange   tomahawk   chocolate   skiing
shampoo   poppadam   typhoon   tangerine

How to play

In each turn you can look up one word from the list at the bottom of the page. If it comes from the language or nationality marked in a square directly connected to the one you are on, show the entry to everyone and move to the new square. If not, keep it to yourself and remember it for later in the game. *Bon voyage!*

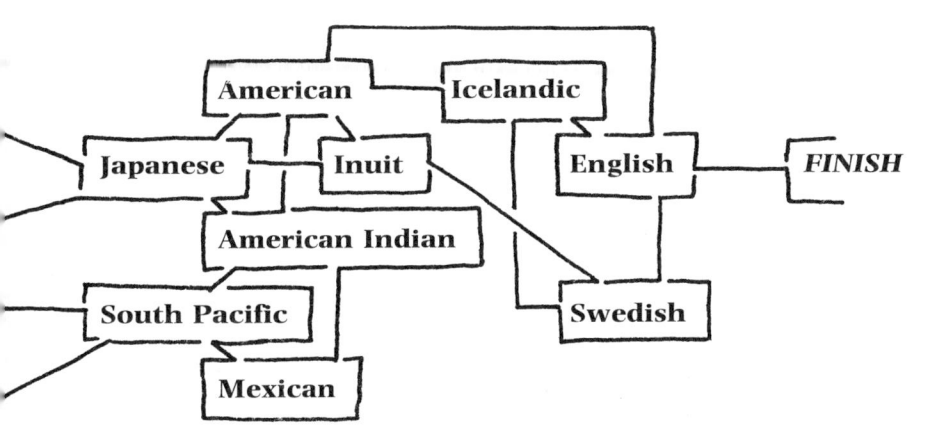

berserk **rucksack** **billabong** **glasnost** **biro**
bikini **rooster** **impala** **kayak** **origami** **apartheid**
tungsten **cheap**

Rules

You may only move along the connecting lines - one square per turn. You may not move to a square which has an opponent's counter on it. You may not write anything down during the game.

Those and These
Nouns and Pronouns

Pronouns are substitute words. They can be used in place of nouns, and are particularly useful to avoid repetition.

The van badly needed a service. *It* hadn't had *one* in years.

1 How would you have to write the second sentence if there were no such words as pronouns?

2 With the help of the entry for **pronoun**, write out a sample set of pronouns, adding, if you can, a few more examples to those given in the dictionary.

pronoun: { ... }

3 Which of the pronouns in your set are plural words?

Which of the pronouns in your set are called *personal* pronouns? Why do you think they are called this?

Which of the pronouns in your set are used to ask questions?

Which of the pronouns in your set are used to point to things or people?

Which of the pronouns in your set are used to express belonging?

Which of the pronouns in your set are old-fashioned words, except in some dialects?

4 Every English noun is either a *he*, a *she*, an *it*, or a *they*.

What **they**, beginning with **n**, is:

(first clue)   an ingredient of soups etc?
(second clue)   cut into narrow strips?
(third clue)   made of pasta?

If you still haven't got it, it begins **noo** ...

There are some more questions like these on the opposite page. Before you start, place a sheet of paper over them so that you can uncover the clues one at a time. Keep your own score: three if you get it right after the first clue, two after the second and one after the third.

He, She, It, or They?
A quiz

1. What *it* beginning with **p** is

   (first clue)   a mixture of lime, sand, and water?
   (second clue)   used for covering walls and ceilings?
   (third clue)   used for setting broken bones?

2. What *she* beginning with **s** is

   (first clue)   a nun?
   (second clue)   a daughter of the same parents as someone else?
   (third clue)   a hospital nurse in charge of others?

3. What *they* beginning with **m**

   (first clue)   are extinct?
   (second clue)   had curved tusks?
   (third clue)   looked like large, hairy elephants?

4. What *it* beginning with **s** is

   (first clue)   a small piece of cork or plastic with a crown of feathers?
   (second clue)   hit with a racket?
   (third clue)   used in a game of badminton?

5. What *it* beginning with **b** is

   (first clue)   bought cheaply?
   (second clue)   a deal?
   (third clue)   an agreement about buying or selling something?

6. What *it* beginning with **s** is

   (first clue)   a country that is under the influence of another more powerful country?
   (second clue)   a moon?
   (third clue)   an object that moves in orbit around a planet?

7. What *it* beginning with **i** is

   (first clue)   an effect produced on the mind?
   (second clue)   a vague idea?
   (third clue)   an imitation of a person's voice or mannerisms?

Top score possible: 21

Adjectives

Look up the meaning of the word **adjective** in the dictionary, and look at the sample adjectives below:

fierce   fine   fragile   formidable   frantic

1   i Which of the sample adjectives could meaningfully fit each of these noun phrases?

a ... line   ... signals
a ... problem   ... opposition
a ... agreement

Some will fit more than one phrase.

ii Can you find five different adjectives all beginning with the same letter, that would fit the same five noun phrases?

2   Many English adjectives have three forms. They are called the **positive**, **comparative** and **superlative**. Look up these words, then copy and complete the table below:

POSITIVE	COMPARATIVE	SUPERLATIVE
big	bigger	biggest
small		
happy		
wide		
heavy		
few		
shy		
good		
bad		
cruel		
stocky		
sad		
much		
many		

Check that you have correctly spelt the comparative and superlative forms, by looking them up.

If no comparative or superlative forms are given in the dictionary, what is the rule for spelling them?

1 Under which headword do each of the following adjectives appear in the dictionary, and which word class does the headword belong to?

mythological   national   progressive   proportional   crinkly

2 i What adjectives are given as derivatives of these headwords:

discern   hypnotize   mutiny   photography   spectre

ii Make up five short sentences to include the five adjectives you have just collected.

3 As well as making up noun phrases, adjectives can also be used as *complements*.

Look up **complement**, especially definition **2**. Which of the two examples of complements that the dictionary gives, is an adjective:

brave or **king of England**?

Complete these sentences with adjectives:

   Some breeds of dogs are … .   The sky looked … .

   The journey seemed … .   The food tasted … .

Check in the dictionary that the complement you have chosen is an adjective.

4 Replace the adjectives in bold with another word or phrase which means the same:

   In many houses the kitchen and bathroom are **communal**.
   My sister was **overwrought**.
   The painting doesn't look **authentic** to me.
   It is dangerous for a referee to appear too **lax**.
   This problem is **perennial**.

Complements
A game for any number of players

Make up a list of nouns or phrases, each followed by the words 'is', 'was', 'are', or 'were'. You can start with the following or make up your own:

School is ...   Washing up is ...   Many people were ...

The oceans are ...   London is ...   The sky was ...

Choose a letter of the alphabet. Ask someone to say 'Go', and write down *a single word*, beginning with that letter, to complement each of the phrases. (You cannot use the same word twice.)

SCHOOL IS BAFFLING

MANY PEOPLE ARE BOWING

LONDON IS BIG

The first to finish says 'Stop,' and earns an extra two points on his or her score. Players take it in turns to read out their completed sentences; if two or more players have chosen the same word, they must cross it out. One point is then scored for every complement that no one else has thought of.

You can use the dictionary. The resulting sentences must make sense.

Adverbs

Adverbs are words which tell us *how*, *when* or *where* something happens.

adverb: {**quickly, carelessly, yesterday, late, here, there**, ...}

Many English adverbs are formed from adjectives by attaching the suffix **-ly**. Usually you just add **-ly** without change, but there are some exceptions.

reliable *adjective* able to be relied on; trustworthy. **reliably** *adverb*, **reliability** *noun*

1 Write down the adverbs that are formed from these adjectives:

   thoughtful   happy   frantic   full   shy   gay   late   preferable

2 A **punctual** person is likely to arrive **punctually**. What sort of person is likely to do the following?

   mix **sociably** with other people
   watch **morosely** whilst other people enjoy themselves
   tidy everything away **fastidiously**
   rush into things **impetuously**
   sneer **contemptuously** at others
   act **magnanimously**

3 Look at the entry for the suffix **-ly** in the Appendix. Which other class of words, besides adverbs, often ends with these letters?

   To which word class does each of the following belong?

   gently   friendly   prickly   purposely   cuddly

Actions

Verbs are sometimes described as action words, but many action words can also be used as nouns.

cough (*say* kof) *verb* send out air from the lungs with a sudden sharp sound.

cough *noun* 1 the act or sound of coughing. 2 an illness that makes you cough.

1 Write two short sentences, one using **cough** as a verb, the other using **cough** as a noun.

2 Which of the following verbs can also be used as nouns?

sneeze   gain   sleep   betray   forget   go   treat   stay

Which of the following nouns can also be used as verbs?

deposit   shadow   paddle   relay   snow   mill   mirror   food

Answer these questions by placing all sixteen words on a Venn diagram.

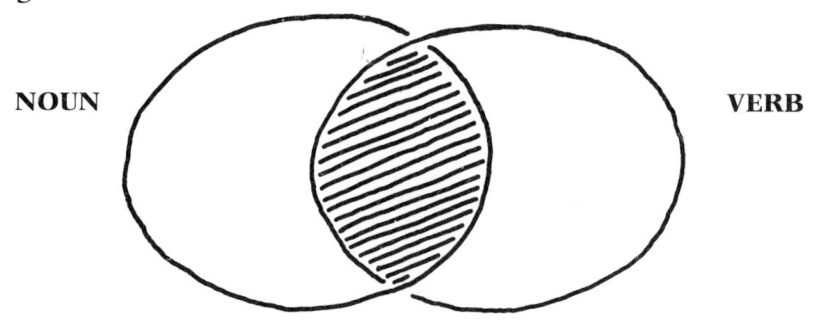

NOUN   VERB

Do some of the words belong in the *intersection* (the shaded part); and if so, why?

3 Many nouns that denote actions are formed from verbs by adding a suffix or changing the spelling.

arrive *verb* > **arrival** *noun*

What nouns are formed from the following verbs?

succeed   descend   deride   refuse   impede   speak   expire   denounce

Use each of the nouns you have collected in a phrase or short sentence.

Feelings

despair *noun* a feeling of hopelessness.
despair *verb* feel despair. [from *de-*, + Latin *sperare* = to hope]

1. The following nouns all denote feelings or emotions. They are listed in a certain order, sometimes called a *spectrum*. Can you see what the order is?

   elation   hope   indifference   pessimism   despair

   Do you think that any of the following extra words belong to the same spectrum, and if so where do they fit in?

   jubilation   ecstasy   misery   despondency   guilt

2. Adjectives can be used to describe how someone feels. For example,

   I felt **desperate**.

   Use adjectives to say how you would be feeling if you were experiencing each of the other nine emotions found in question 1.

Group work: Miming

Write each of the words in the box below on a small piece of paper and fold it. Give one to each person. (There may be some left over for a second round.)

If you don't know its meaning, look up your word in the dictionary; then mime it for the others, who must try to identify which word is yours. They too may consult the dictionary if they want to.

Points: Plus-one for a correct identification. Minus-one for an incorrect guess.

| irascible | desolate | snubbed | impassive | dejected |
| circumspect | harassed | impetuous | reticent | exhilarated |

When these words have run out, try finding some more of your own. As well as the dictionary, a *thesaurus* could help you find new words for this activity.

True or False?
A quiz

Decide, or guess, whether each of these statements is true or false. Then use the dictionary to find out if you were right.

1. The word **jamb**, meaning a side post of a doorway or window frame, comes from the French word for a leg.
2. **laconic** and **terse** are synonyms.
3. An **interval** was originally the space between ramparts on a fortress.
4. **liberal** and **library** have the same root and origin.
5. The five-line verses called **limericks** were named after a German poet.
6. **lavish**, meaning generous, used to mean a downpour of rain.
7. **liquid** and **liquorice** come from the same Latin root.
8. **maelstrom** means whirlpool.
9. **molars**, the big teeth at the back of the jaw, are named after millstones.
10. **parasite** once meant 'guest at a meal'.
11. A **steeplechase** is so called because the race originally had a church steeple in view as a goal.
12. A **tactician** is someone who shows a lot of tact.
13. **Koala** bears are found only in Africa.
14. **krill** is the name of a tiny fish.
15. The word **trek**, meaning travel a long way on foot, comes from Alaska in the USA.

What's the Connection?
A quiz

Can you discover, from the dictionary, some connection between the following pairs of words or things?

1 a rainbow and an iris

2 a washing line and a linen sheet

3 an officer in command of a regiment and the inside part of a nut

4 the words island and insulation

5 insect larvae and ghosts

6 applause and an explosion

7 a tail and a queue

8 state of Utopia and nowhere

9 tallness and swiftness

10 an interlude and a game

11 a planet and a wanderer

12 silage and missiles

13 chess and a former ruler of Iran

14 the words business and pigeon

15 a Tory and an outlaw

New Words

Some words are very old: they go so far back that no one can be sure of the exact origins. But some words have come into our language quite recently.

1. Look up the word **chauvinism**. What did it mean originally, and what does it mean now? What is the approximate age of the word?

    two hundred years   five hundred years   a thousand years

2. **motel**, **moped** and **smog** are new English words made by combining two existing words. What are the words that have been combined in each case?

    Can you think of some other words that have been formed in this way?

3. The following words name or describe new objects:

    slot-machine   hamburger   juke-box   keyboard   T-shirt

    high-rise   turnstile   torpedo   disco   barbecue

    Try to find out, or guess, how each of these words originated.

4. Many new words have been constructed out of old parts. What do the following words mean and what do their parts mean?

    television   parachute   aqualung   locomotive   transistor

    photograph   minibus   supermarket   contraflow   microchip

5. Some words are shortenings of older or longer words. What are the full versions of these?

    pram   bus   taxi   bike   fridge   zoo

New words and expressions are being invented all the time to describe new events or activities. Some of these are old words that have been given new life, for example, **poll tax**.

Some are foreign words that have become part of everyday life, for example, **kebab**.

Some are words that have been made from others, for example, **trainers** (from training shoes).

Some are spelt from the initials of a phrase, for example **radar**.

Discussion and group work

Can you think of any other new words, especially words that you or your friends use? Do you know, or can you guess, how these words originated?

The word **phoney** is given as having an unknown origin. What do you think its origin might have been? Discuss various possibilities and then make up your own dictionary entry for this word.

Invent a word of your own and write a complete dictionary entry for it. There is a checklist below to help you.

Try to make the word seem genuine: in other words give it a sound, a meaning, and an explanation which could belong to a real word. Who knows, it might catch on!

Headword
Pronunciation
Word class
Definition
Derivates
Example
Phrases
Notes on usage
Origin

See if anyone can guess the meaning of your word. Tell them some of the details, but leave out the definition.

Answers

Page 2

1. **Saffron** is used to colour or flavour food.
2. **Safari** comes from Arabic.
3. **Derv** stands for 'diesel-engined road vehicle'.
4. The **hock** is the middle joint of an animal's hind leg.
5. The winter **solstice** is around 22 December.
6. An **osteopath** treats certain diseases by manipulating a person's bones and muscles.
7. You would be unwise as a **noxious** drink would be unpleasant and harmful.
8. A **magnolia** tree has large white or pale-pink flowers.
9. *Deinos* means terrible and *sauros* means lizard (from Ancient Greek).
10. **Mah-jong** is a game for four people.
11. A **Catherine wheel** is named after St Catherine, who was martyred on a spiked wheel.
12. ii.
13. *Insure*. The correct word is *ensure*.
14. **September** is from the latin word for seven *septem*, because it was the seventh month in the ancient Roman calendar.
15. i **Finns**   ii **Ghanaians**   iii **Cypriots**

Page 3

1. The *definition* tells you what the headword means.
   The *word class* tells you what sort of word the headword is.
   The *origin* tells you where the word came from.
   The list of *derivatives* gives you other words which are close to the headword in spelling and meaning.
2. Take entries from dictionary and treat them as **alphabet**.

Page 4

1. accost   adopt   chin   fist   ghost   know
2. maximum   meeting   motion   mutiny   mystery
   parade   pleasure   poetry   predict   punctual
   slack   sleepy   slender   slippery   slow
   theirs   them   then   these   they

Page 6

1 **mainland** *noun* the main part of a country or continent, not the islands round it.

obstacle *noun* something that stands in the way or obstructs progress.

conquer *verb* defeat; overcome.

fish *noun* an animal that lives and breathes in water.

seven *noun & adjective* the number 7; one more than six.

grey *noun* the colour between black and white; like ashes.

2 **harsh** (2)   **dry** (4)   **abuse** (3)   **explode** (3)   **follow** (6)   **out** (5)

Page 7

1 The dictionary gives **bat** as an example of a homograph.

A *homograph* is a word that is spelt like another but has a different meaning or origin, and a *homophone* is a word that has the same sound as another.

2 **bass** (2)   **batten** (2)   **bay** (4)   **fell** (3)   **felt** (2)   **sound** (4)   **lay** (4)

3 Homographs: **deal** and **hind**

Page 8

definite   Fix a definite time.
             Is it definite that we are to move?

makeshift   We used a box as a makeshift table.

other *adjective*   some other tune.
                       Try the other shoe.
                       my other friends.
                       I saw him the other day.

virtual   His silence was a virtual admission of guilt.

zoom   Prices had zoomed.

Page 10

1 **old** *adjective*   **ocean** *noun*   **often** *adverb*   **operate** *verb*

or *conjunction*   **oh** *interjection*   **OPEC** *abbreviation*

2 nouns

3 verbs

Page 11

5 **lift** (2)   **limit** (2)   **little** (2)   **light**^{1} (3)   **light**^{2} (2)

6 i **fireman**   ii **fear** or **fancy**   iii **fancy**

64

7

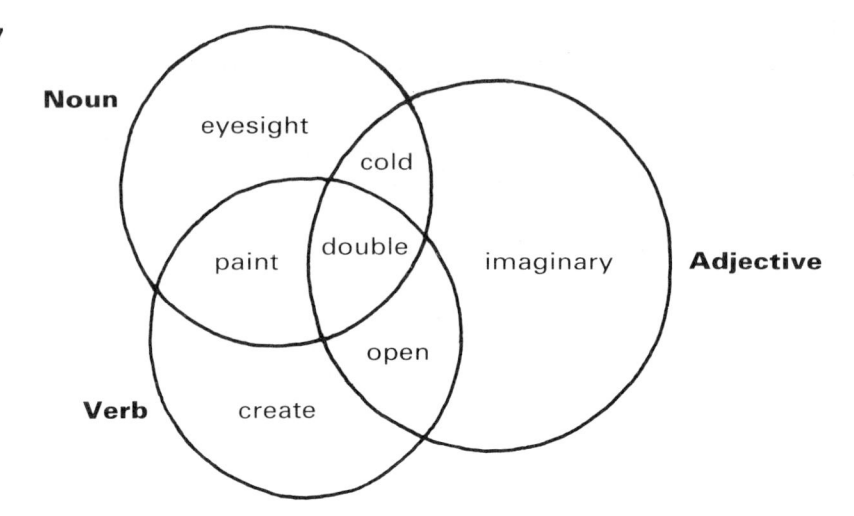

[Venn diagram with three overlapping circles labeled Noun, Verb, and Adjective:]
- Noun only: eyesight
- Noun ∩ Adjective: cold
- Noun ∩ Verb: paint
- Noun ∩ Verb ∩ Adjective: double
- Adjective only: imaginary
- Verb ∩ Adjective: open
- Verb only: create

8 **home** (4) *noun, adjective, adverb, verb*   **test** (2) *noun, verb*
sound (3) *noun, verb, adjective*   **east** (3) *noun, adjective, adverb*
run (2) *verb, noun*

Page 13

1 *singular*: **town**   river   girl   friend   nose   cradle   computer
plural: **horses**   shoes   engines   politicians

The plural forms have an **-s** at the end.

singular

2   churches   ferries   calves   wives   spies   teeth   potatoes   helices   children   aircraft   formulae   fish (or fishes)

Both, because the plural forms are irregular.

3   They have no singular form.

4 *singular*: **dahlia**   fuchsia   *plural*: **criteria**   media   bacteria

Page 14

2   called, calling   stayed, staying   worked, working
expressed, expressing   intended, intending

3   exploded, exploding   stopped, stopping   planned, planning
cried, crying   compelled, compelling

4   came, coming   ran, running   wept, weeping
slept, sleeping   fought, fighting

5   benefited, benefiting   brought, bringing
committed, committing   limited, limiting
managed, managing

Regular: **benefit**   limit

Page 15

1 ate, eaten   woke, woken   wrote, written   spoke, spoken
did, done

3 flapping   skiing   replying   shining   damaging

4 think   challenge   win   smile   rise

Page 16

2 cyclist   instructor   inventor   grumbler   groveller competitor   correspondent   representative   applicant entrant

3 i   magnificence
orphaned
totally   explanation
perilously
historical importance
intensification   hostilities
initiation

   ii **magnificent** *adjective* > **magnificence** *noun*
orphan *noun* > **orphaned** *adjective*
total *adjective* > **totally** *adverb*
explain *verb* > **explanation** *noun*
perilous *adjective* > **perilously** *adverb*
history *noun* > **historical** *adjective*
important *adjective* > **importance** *noun*
intensify *verb* > **intensification** *noun*
hostile *adjective* > **hostilities** *noun*
initiate *verb* > **initiation** *noun*

Page 17

2 **cough** (1)   **initiative** (4)   **jeopardy** (3)   **courier** (3) **indubitable** (5)

3 i-**on**-osphere   medi-**e**-val   in-**ex**-orable   pro-**gress** (verb) **pro**-gress (noun)

Page 18

1 make off = go away quickly
on the move = moving; making progress
get your own back = have your revenge
come by = obtain
behind a person's back = kept secret from him or her deceitfully
back out = refuse to do what was agreed
play down = give people the impression that something is not important
take in good part = not to be offended at something
in person = being actually present oneself
on hand = available

Page 19

1 You must learn to curb your impatience.
The strange craft was glowing in alternate colours.
Being in Scotland at the time of the murder gave me an alibi.
This time the sound was quite distinct.
There have been tales of strange phenomena at the house.
Part of his disguise was a luxuriant black beard.
My grandmother is a compulsive supporter of Liverpool F.C.
Inflammable gases are a danger in coal mines.

Page 21

1 **denim** (*French*)   **finish** (*Latin*)   **sugar** (*Arabic*)   **melody** (*Greek*)
billycan (*Australian*)   **bride** (*Old English*)   **butler** (*Old French*)
potato (*South American*)   **kiosk** (*Persian*)   **mammoth** (*Russian*)

2 They all originate from the names of the men who discovered them:
A. Dahl, Louis Braille, Duke of Wellington, Earl of Cardigan, Earl of Sandwich, J. P. Joule

3 **deadline**   (originally this meant a line round an American military prison; if a prisoner went beyond it he could be shot)

juggernaut   (named after a Hindu god whose image was dragged in procession on a huge wheeled vehicle)

lord   (person who keeps the bread)

truncheon   (from Latin *truncus* = tree-trunk)

laser   (from the initials of 'light amplification (by) stimulated emission (of) radiation')

harass   (from the Old French *harer* = to set the dog on someone)

thug   (the Thugs were robbers in India in the 17th–19th centuries)

robot   (from Czech *robota* = compulsory labour)

tulip   (from Old Turkish *tuliband* = turban – because the flowers are this shape)

tadpole   (from old words, *tad* = toad + *poll* = head)

poll tax   (tax on each person, *poll* = head)

dodo   (from Portuguese *doudo* = fool)

4 Origin: *littera*

Others: *liber*
mortis
battuere
vindicta
signum

Page 22

1 A prefix is placed at the beginning of a word to alter its meaning or to form a new word.

*hex*agon   *omni*vorous   *dis*traction   *uni*verse   *peri*scope

2 A suffix is placed at the end of a world to form another word or to form a plural, past tense, comparative, superlative, etc.

dem*ocracy*   high*est*   clock*wise*   mus*ician*   tele*pathy*

3 *ad nauseam* (Latin) = until people are sick of it

doppelgänger (German) = the ghost of a living person

laissez-faire (French) = a government's policy of not interfering

hara-kiri (Japanese) = a form of suicide formerly used by Japanese officers when in disgrace

sotto voce (Italian) = in a very quiet voice

eureka (Greek) = I have found it!

faux pas (French) = an embarrassing blunder

bona fide = (Latin) = genuine; without fraud

4 They are based on those given by the ancient Romans and are named after the planets.

5 They are based on those given by the ancient Romans.

6 An American pint is lighter (16 fluid oz) than a British pint (20 fluid oz).

7 30 °C

Page 23

1 Heave   **2** Faint, Close

Page 25

2
hangar	shed	place where aircraft are kept
mead	alcoholic drink	made from honey and water
crocus	plant	has yellow, purple, or white flowers
gondola	boat	has high pointed ends and is used on canals in Venice
thirteen	number	one more than twelve

3 plant, fungus, mushroom   animal, gastropod, snail
communication, talk, gossip   sustenance, offal, liver
matter, mineral, metal, zinc   study, science, biology, botany

Page 26

1 near   fact   convex   proud   generous

2 unusual   infrequent   inexpensive   unprejudiced   insane

3 unusual = exceptional
infrequent = not often
inexpensive = cheap
unprejudiced = impartial
insane = mad

4 **anticlimax** (= a disappointing ending or result) climax

nonsense (= words put together in a way that does not mean anything) sense

irrelevant (= not relevant) relevant

immobile (= not moving) mobile

posterior (= situated at the back of something) anterior

5 **minimum**
evergreen
introvert
adding
agreement
irregular
ascending

Page 28

1 dog (bitch) count (countess) cob (pen) paternal (maternal) fox (vixen) masculine (feminine) sire (dam) nephew (niece) drone (queen)

2 steward hero manager brotherly horseman fiancé masculinity Knight bridegroom

3 cock, hen brother, sister king, queen father, mother colt, filly

Page 29

1 A word made of two or more parts.

2 **Simple**: water fall break
Compound: waterfall breakwater

4 life-jacket lighthouse mainland
sandpaper set-up nanny-goat
framework lift-off pickpocket

Page 30

1 about fifty

2 national

change planetary view dependent

3 **multi-** (*many*) multicoloured, multilateral
mono- (*one; single*) monochrome, monogamy
equi- (*equal*) equilateral, equivalent

semi- (*half; partly*) semicircle, semiquaver
poly- (*many*) polygamy, polygon

4 i 1 under   2 subordinate, secondary

   ii suc- succession
       suf- suffix
       sur- surrender
       sus- suspend

Page 31

2 hopeful   merciful   useful   mindful
   thoughtless   harmless

3 laziest   explosive   intention   purification   telephonist

4 plant   meditate   official
   mortal   solid   script

Page 32

1 impress   impressive   impression
   depress   depressive   depression
   compress   compression   pressure
   suppress   suppression
   express   expressive   expression

2 **suspend** hang   **subtract**   deduct; take away
   collect bring together **effect**   produce
   predict forecast   **intersect** cut across
   defend   resist attack **suppose**   think so
   attempt try   **provoke**   anger

3 cor**rupt**ion   dis**rupt**ion   **rupt**ure   inter**rupt**
   im**port**   ex**port**   **port**er   sup**port**er   **port**able   re**port**er
   pre**fer**ence   con**fer**ence   inter**fer**ence

Page 33

1 production   procession   extension   expulsion   invasion
   reception   admission

2 exclusive   destructive   explosive   defensive   excessive
   deceptive

3 ii retracts
       attracts
       extracts

4 i twisting, especially of one end of a thing while the other is held in a fixed position

   ii ex**tort**ionist
       con**tort**ionist
       torturer

Page 35

1 I don't want to *see* you here again.
She suddenly *saw* something out of the corner of her eye.
We haven't *seen* him around here recently.
I'll be *seeing* you.
I honestly don't know what she *sees* in him.

2 seven (am, are, is; was, were; been, being)

3 as the object of a verb or after a preposition

5 these women   those men

Page 36

1 Celtic

2 Anglo-Saxons (Old English or Anglo-Saxon)
Vikings (Old Norse)
Normans (Middle English)

3 Under the Anglo-Saxons the country became 'England' or 'land of the Angles' and from it came 'Englisc' or English.

4 i Celtic: **Carlisle**, **Thames**, **Avon**, etc.
ii Anglo-Saxon: **eat**, **drink**, **sleep**, etc.
iii Norse: **scare**, **scrap**, **skirt**, etc.
iv Norman French: **advise**, **command**, **court**, etc.

Page 37

1 **manacle, manicure, manipulate, manoevre, manual**, etc.

2 They all come from the Latin root *fac* = make.

3 They are all shapes and originate from Greek.

4 **Algebra** is from Arabic. **Geometry** and **arithmetic** are from Greek.

5 **alligator**   (from Spanish *el lagarto* = the lizard)

bonfire   (from *bone fire* = a fire to dispose of people's or animals' bones)

budget   (from French *bouge* = leather bag)

derrick   (originally meant 'a gallows', named after Derrick, a London hangman in about 1600)

meteor   (from Greek *meteoros* = high in the air)

malaria   (from Italian *mala aria* = bad air, which was once thought to cause the disease)

mayday   (from French *m'aider* = help me)

mousse   (from French = froth)

nausea   (originally 'sea-sickness', from Greek *naus* = ship)

racket   (from Arabic *rahat* = palm of the hand)

6 **adder** (originally called *a nadder*, which became *an adder*)

orange (from Persian *narang*)

nickname (originally *a neke name* from *an eke-name* (*eke* = addition, + *name*)

7 **tantalize** (from the name of Tantalus in Greek mythology, who was punished by being made to stand near water and fruit which moved away when he tried to reach them)

lynch (named after William Lynch, an American judge who allowed this type of punishment in about 1780)

tawdry (from *St Audrey's lace* (cheap finery formerly sold at St Audrey's fair at Ely))

marathon (named after Marathon in Greece, from which a messenger ran to Athens in 490 BC to announce that Greeks had defeated the Persian army)

Page 40

1 **father** (*faeder*)   **mother** (*modor*)   **brother** (*brothor*)

husband (*husbonda*)   **bride** (*bryd*)

2 i The original meaning of **lord** was 'person who keeps the bread' and of **lady** 'person who makes the bread'. Nowadays, **lord** refers to a nobleman who is allowed to use the title 'Lord' in front of his name, and **lady** refers to any well-mannered woman or a woman of a good social position.

ii The Old English words for **well**[1] and **well**[2] were *wella* and *wel* and not homographs. The Old English words for **barrow**[1] and **barrow**[2] were *bearwe* and *beorg* and not homographs.

iii The Old English words for **barn** were *bere ern* meaning barley-house.

Page 42

1 Middle English (spoken by the ordinary people) and French (spoken by the Norman ruling classes).

2 advise, command, court, govern, people, reign, etc.

Page 44

1 i French used by Normans came from Latin, all scholars used Latin, expansion of Holy Roman Empire, spread of Christianity, European interest in Greek and Roman culture.

ii See above.

iii From the Anglo-Saxons who lived on fringes of Roman Empire.

2 **interim** (English = temporary; Latin = meanwhile)

posterior (English = buttocks; Latin = further back)

minimum (English = lowest possible number; Latin = least thing)

omnibus (English = a bus; Latin = for everybody)

extra (English = additional person or thing; Latin = outside)

3 **formulae** (set of chemical symbols showing what a substance consists of)

curricula (courses of study)

opera (numbered musical compositions)

genera (groups of similar animals or plants)

fungi (plants without leaves or flowers that grow on other plants or on decayed material)

4 In Latin **plus** means more and **minus** means less.

5 **ego** (Latin = I; now = a person's self or self-respect)

exit (Latin = he or she goes out; now = the way out of a building)

ludo (Latin = I play; now = a game played with dice and counters on a board)

circus (Latin = ring; now = a travelling show with clowns, acrobats, animals, etc)

campus (Latin = field); now: the grounds of a university or college)

video (Latin = I see; now = recorded or broadcast pictures)

6 As a thousand paces

Page 45

1 i 10
ii circumnavigate
circumscribe
circumvent
circumference
circumstances

2 correct, rectitude, rectify, rectangle, rectilinear, rector, etc.

3 **progress** = forward movement (going forwards)
aggression = starting an attack or war (going into war)
congress = conference (going together)
regression = backward movement (going backwards)

progress and **regression**

Page 46

1 The Renaissance took place in the 14th-16th centuries when Europeans became interested in Greek literature, philosophy, art, and buildings, thus introducing Greek terms into English.

2   **atmosphere** = the air around the earth (from Greek *atmos* = vapour + *sphaira* = ball)

3   **comedy** = play or film that makes people laugh (from Greek *komos* = merry-making + *oide* = song)

   tragedy = play with unhappy events or sad ending (from Greek *tragos* = goat + *oide* = song)

   theatre = a building where plays, etc. are performed to an audience (from Greek *theatron* = a place for seeing things)

4   forms names of descriptive sciences (e.g. geography) or methods of writing and drawing, etc. (from Greek *-graphia* = writing)

   photography, calligraphy, cartography, etc.

5   **biology, zoology, theology, psychology, terminology**, etc. (from Greek *logia* = to study)

6   8. *Physis* = nature; *physikos* = natural

7   They are all words associated with medicine.

   autopsy (from Greek *autopsia* = seeing with your own eyes)
   anaesthetic (from Greek *an* = without + *aisthesis* = sensation)
   physiotherapy (from Greek *physis* = nature + *therapeia* = healing)
   antibiotic (from Greek *anti-* = against + *bios* = life)
   pathology (from Greek *pathos* = suffering + *-logia* = to study)

   biopsy, antidote, anorexia, anthropology, antithesis, etc.

Page 47

1   **module** = an independent part of a spacecraft, building, etc.
   capsule = a compartment that can be separated from the rest of a spacecraft

   astronaut = a person who travels in a spacecraft
   shuttle = a train, bus, or aircraft that makes frequent short journeys between two points

2   They all belong to computer science.

   software = computer programs, tapes, etc.
   hardware = the machinery of a computer
   byte = a fixed number of bits (= binary digits) in a computer, often representing a single character
   VDU = visual display unit
   floppy disk = a flexible disk holding data for use in a computer

3   **windsurfing** = surfing on a board that has a sail fixed to it
   hang-gliding = using a framework to glide through the air
   skateboarding = riding on a small board with wheels while standing

4   **acid rain** = rain made acid by mixing with waste gases from factories, etc.
   plutonium = a radioactive substance used in nuclear weapons and reactors

ozone layer = a layer of ozone high in the atmosphere, protecting the world from harmful amounts of the sun's rays
asbestos = a soft fireproof material
radioactivity = atoms breaking up and sending out radiation which produces electrical and chemical effects and penetrates things

5   **nylon** = a synthetic, lightweight, very strong cloth or fibre
    polymers = substances whose molecules are formed from a large number of simple molecules combined
    polystyrene = a kind of plastic used for insulating or packing things
    vinyl = a kind of plastic
    melamine = a strong kind of plastic

6   They are all named after their discoverers: James Watt, A. M. Ampere, J. P. Joule, H. R. Hertz, A. Celsius.

7   **science** (from Latin *scientia* = knowledge)
    technology (from Greek *techne* = skill + *-logia* = study)
    physics (from Greek *physikos* = natural)
    chemistry (from Arabic *alkimiya* = the art of changing metals)
    atomic (from Greek *atomos* = indivisible)
    zoology (from Greek *zoion* = animal + *-logia* = study)

Page 48–49

amok (Malay)	**battalion** (Italian)	**cherish** (French)
magazine (Arabic)	**pyjamas** (Urdu)	**barracks** (Spanish)
orange (Persian)	**tomahawk** (American Indian)	
chocolate (Mexican)	**skiing** (Norwegian)	**shampoo** (Hindu)
poppadam (Tamil)	**typhoon** (Chinese)	**tangerine** (Moroccan)
berserk (Icelandic)	**rucksack** (German)	**billabong** (Australian)
glasnost (Russian)	**biro** (Hungarian)	**bikini** (South Pacific)
rooster (American)	**impala** (Zulu)	**kayak** (Inuit)
origami (Japanese)	**apartheid** (Afrikaans)	**tungsten** (Swedish)
cheap (English)		

Page 50

1   The van hadn't had a service in years.

3   these, those, we, us, theirs, etc.

    I, me, we, us, thou, thee, you, ye, etc.
    (because they concern a particular person)

    who? what? which? etc.

    this, that, these, those

    mine, yours, theirs, etc.

    thou, thee, ye, etc.

4   noodle

Page 51

1. plaster 2. sister 3. mammoths 4. shuttlecock
5. bargain 6. satellite 7. impression

Page 52

1. i a fine line
      a formidable problem
      a fragile agreement
      frantic signals
      fierce opposition

   ii single sizeable secure strange strong

2.
small	smaller	smallest	**bad**	worse	worst
happy	happier	happiest	**cruel**	crueller	cruellest
wide	wider	widest	**stocky**	stockier	stockiest
heavy	heavier	heaviest	**sad**	sadder	saddest
few	fewer	fewest	**much**	more	most
shy	shyer	shyest	**many**	more	most
good	better	best			

Page 53

1. **mythology** *noun*   **nation** *noun*   **progress** *verb*
   proportion *noun*   **crinkle** *verb*

2. i discerning   hypnotic   mutinous   photographic
      spectral

3. brave

Page 55

1. thoughtfully   happily   frantically   fully   shyly
   gaily   lately   preferably

2. sociable   morose   fastidious   impetuous
   contemptuous   magnanimous

3. adjectives

   gently *adverb*   **friendly** *adjective*   **prickly** *adjective*
   purposely *adverb*   **cuddly** *adjective*

Page 56

2. sneeze   gain   sleep   go   treat   stay
   deposit   shadow   paddle   relay   snow   mill   mirror

```
              Noun    sneeze    Verb
                      gain
                      sleep
                      go
                      treat
              food    stay     betray
                      deposit  forget
                      shadow
                      paddle
                      relay
                      snow
                      mill
                      mirror
```

Some of the words are both verbs and nouns.

3 succession   descent   derision   refusal
    impediment   speech   expiry   denunciation

Page 57

1 They range from one extreme of emotion (**elation**) through to another (**despair**).

   jubilation   elation   hope   indifference
   pessimism   misery   despair

2 elated   hopeful   indifferent   pessimistic   jubilant
    ecstatic   miserable   despondent   guilty

Page 58

1 True   **2** True   **3** True   **4** False   **5** False   **6** True
7 False   **8** True   **9** True   **10** True   **11** True
12 False   **13** False   **14** True   **15** False

Page 59

1 Iris comes from the Greek word for **rainbow**
2 **line** comes from Latin *linea* = linen thread
3 colonel is pronounced **ker**-nel, like the inside of the nut
4 both come from Latin *insula* = island
5 **larvae** comes from Latin = ghost, mask
6 both come from Latin *plaudere*
7 **queue** comes from Latin *cauda* = tail
8 **Utopia** means 'Nowhere'
9 the original meaning of **tallness** was 'swift'
10 **interlude** comes from *inter-*, + Latin *ludus* = game

11 **planet** comes from Greek *planetes* = wanderer

12 **silage** is connected to **silo** which can also be an underground place for storing a **missile**

13 **chess** comes from Persian *shah* = king; the *Shah of Iran* was a former ruler

14 **pigeon** can mean 'a person's business or responsibility' as in *That's your pigeon*.

15 **Tory** was originally used of Irish outlaws

Page 60

1 **chauvinism** = prejudiced belief that your own group, country, etc. is superior to others (from the name of Nicholas Chauvin, a French soldier under Napoleon, noted for his extreme patriotism)

   two hundred years

2 **motor** and **hotel**   **motor** and **pedal**   **smoke** and **fog**

4 **television** = a system using radio waves to reproduce a view of scenes, events, or plays, etc. on a screen (from Greek *tele-* = far off + Latin *visum* = seen)

   parachute = an expanding device on which people or things can float slowly to the ground from an aircraft (from Italian *para* = defend + French *chute* = a fall)

   aqualung = a diver's portable breathing-apparatus, with cylinders of compressed air connected to a face-mask (from Latin *aqua* = water + *lung*)

   locomotive = a railway engine (from Latin *locus* = place + *motivus* = moving)

   transistor = a tiny semiconductor device controlling a flow of electricity (from **trans**fer from Latin *trans-* = across + *ferre* = carry and re**sistor** = a device that increases the resistance to an electric current)

   photograph = a picture made by the effect of light or other radiation on film or special paper (from Greek *photo-* = of light and *-graphia* = writing)

   minibus = a very small bus (from mini = miniature + bus = a large vehicle for passengers to travel in)

   supermarket = a large self-service shop that sells food and other goods (from Latin *super-* = over + *merx* = merchandise)

   contraflow = a flow of traffic travelling in the opposite direction to the usual flow and close beside it (from Latin *contra-* = against + flow = a flowing movement or mass)

   microchip = a very small piece of silicon, etc. made to work like a complex wired electric circuit (from Greek *mikros* = very small + chip = a thin piece cut or broken off something hard)

5 **perambulator**   **omnibus**   **taximeter cab**   **bicycle**
   refrigerator   **zoological gardens**

Oxford University Press, Walton Street, Oxford OX2 6DP

OXFORD NEW YORK TORONTO
DELHI BOMBAY CALCUTTA MADRAS KARACHI
KUALA LUMPUR SINGAPORE HONG KONG TOKYO
NAIROBI DAR ES SALAAM CAPE TOWN
MELBOURNE AUCKLAND MADRID

and associated companies in
BERLIN IBADAN

Oxford is a trade mark of Oxford University Press

© John Butterworth 1992
First published 1992
10 9 8 7 6 5 4 3 2 1

All rights reserved. No part of this publication may be reproduced, stored in a retrieval system, or transmitted, in any form or by any means, without the prior permission in writing of Oxford University Press. Within the UK, exceptions are allowed in respect of any fair dealing for the purpose of research or private study, or criticism or review, as permitted under the Copyright, Designs and Patents Act, 1988, or in the case of reprographic reproduction in accordance with the terms of the licences issued by the Copyright Licensing Agency. Enquiries concerning reproduction outside these terms and in other countries should be sent to the Rights Department, Oxford University Press, at the address above

This book is sold subject to the condition that it shall not, by way of trade or otherwise, be lent, re-sold, hired out, or otherwise circulated without the publisher's prior consent in any form of binding or cover other than that in which it is published and without a similar condition including this condition being imposed on the subsequent purchaser

ISBN 0 19 910280 5

Printed in Great Britain by BPCC Hazells Ltd, Aylesbury

The Best of CaféLit 5

The Best of CaféLit 5

an anthology

Edited by Gill James

Chapeltown Books

This collection copyright © Chapeltown Books 2016. Copyright in the text reproduced herein remains the property of the individual authors, and permission to publish is gratefully acknowledged by the editors and publishers.

All rights reserved

No parts of this publication may be reproduced, stored in a retrieval system, or transmitted in any form or by any means, electronic, mechanical, photocopying, recording or otherwise without prior permission of the copyright owner.

British Library Cataloguing in Publication Data

A Record of this Publication is available from the British Library

ISBN 978-1-910542-04-0

This edition published 2016 by Chapeltown Books
Manchester, England

All Chapeltown books are published on paper derived from sustainable resources.

Contents

Foreword	8
The Fledgling *Tania Sharman*	10
Dead Quiet *Alan Cadman*	11
Fatal Flaws *Jenny Palmer*	13
Filling the Space *Helen Laycock*	18
Hot Chocolate Day *Vanessa Horn*	20
Slippery Slope *Penny Rogers*	25
MONG *Neil Campbell*	28
Perseverance *Paul Westgate*	33
Bad *Mary Bevan*	34
Shark Bait *Susan A Eames*	35
Jigsaw *Debz Hobbs-Wyatt*	38
Head Banging *Sue Cross*	40

Paris *Roger Noons*	45
New Term *Gill James*	46
Never Again! *Janet Bunce*	47
Monday Morning *Roger Noons*	48
Josie The Spy *David Deanshaw*	49
Web-based Artist *Mike Olley*	54
Dialling 999 *Vicky Jacobson*	55
For The Love of Harley *Eleanor Patrick*	60
Sex and Socks and Rock 'n' Roll *Susan A. Eames*	73
Scarf Girl *Penny Rogers*	76
Scream *Roger Noons*	81
Wake up Call *Linda Flynn*	82
An Alternative Nativity *Laura van Weegen*	86
Santaphobia *Susan A. Eames*	90

The Chimes At Midnight *Paula R C Readman*	93
Christmas on the High Street *Dawn Knox*	105
Telling The Time *Allison Symes*	106
Night Shift *B. Lieve*	107
On Repeat *James Phillips*	108
Index Of Drinks	112
Writing For CaféLit	113

Foreword

It has been my great privilege this year to make the selection for The Best of CaféLit 5. This meant reading every single story on the web site and then selecting the very best to be put into this little anthology that is available both as a print book and as an e-book. What a joy that was but also what a difficult task: all of the stories that make it on to the web site are good and of course all of these have already gone through an editorial process so they're quite polished.

I've been asked recently to define what makes a good CaféLit story. That's a tricky question. I suppose the bottom line is it has to be something you can take in whilst you're in a café. We hope that you'll select your story according to your mood and that the assigned drink will help you with that.

One writer informed us at our annual get-together last year that assigning the drink was the most difficult part but that when she worked the other way round – thought of a drink first and then made up the story to go with it, it all worked much better.

We have longer stories and shorter stories. We have ones that we hope will make you laugh, others that will make you cry and yet more that will make you think. Some too have car chase moments and will keep you on the edge of your seat. Some writers have experimented with form and demand a little more of the reader. Whichever story you choose to accompany your cuppa we're sure it will stay with you for some time. That is the beauty of the short story. It invites readers to be a little more proactive than they are when reading a novel.

We welcome back some known writers who have appeared in earlier Best of CaféLit publications. We are also delighted to welcome some newcomers.

Popular as ever are our 100-worders and indeed this volume starts off with one. These short sharp pieces of prose contain masses of story. We're looking at supplying these as well on mouse mats, coasters, T-shirts, bags etc.

CaféLit supports the work of the Creative Café Project. Half of the profit from the books is shared by authors and the other half goes in the Project.

The Creative Café Project is about identifying and supporting cafés which provide a space where creative practitioners can interact with their audiences and peers. Take a look here:
http://www.creativecafeproject.org

The Fledgling
Tania Sharman

The Goldeneye – Smooth cocktail made from rum and pineapple juice. Served with a wedge of pineapple.

Jonathan believed that he could fly.

He would often feel himself becoming lighter and lighter, until he was lifted up into the sky where he would then swoop and soar on the air currents.

'That boy is too much in his head, constantly daydreaming,' complained his father bitterly.

'Put your coat on Jonathan, we are going shopping,' said his mother.

They walked to the street corner, where his mother stopped and chatted to a neighbour.

'Come along Jonathan,' she said, turning to her son. But all that remained were a few feathers on the pavement where he had once stood.

About the Author
Tania Sharman lives in Chingford in East London. Most of her time at the moment is spent in the production of a pantomime on behalf of her Local Theatre Company. This includes lots of designing of artwork, prop making, and putting together choreography. She has always entertained the idea of being able to write a story. This is only her second 100 word piece that she has written and submitted to CaféLit.

Dead Quiet
Alan Cadman

A mug of hot sweet tea

He stepped out of the car unimpressed. 'What's that awful smell?'

'That, my dear,' his wife replied in a theatrical voice, 'is the aroma of the countryside.'

'It smells more like horse—'

'Look around at all these wonderful views. You're going to love it here.'

'But we are townies,' he said, pinching his nose. 'I would hate to live in this house, it's dead quiet and where is that bloody estate agent?'

She pushed the front door; it creaked open. She reeled back. 'You're right about it being dead quiet. He's on the floor and he is quite dead.'

About the Author
After being diagnosed with Multiple Sclerosis in 2000, Alan took up creative writing as a hobby. He has been writing short stories for nine years. Before that he was the editor of a civic society newsletter for a short while, but had to give it up due to health problems.

In 2011 Alan made the short list for one story and became a prize winner for flash fiction. He also won first prize, of £100, in a poetry competition in 2013. The three accolades were awarded by the same best-selling UK magazine for writers. In 2014 a story of his was included in an international anthology of twenty ghost stories; published in paperback and e-reader. Alan doesn't write as much as he would like to, due to varying issues, but hopes to continue for as long as he can.

Fatal Flaws
Jenny Palmer
Tea; gone cold

When the face appeared on her Facebook page, Ann was taken aback. She had recently, and regrettably, extended her privacy settings. Now she was receiving posts from all and sundry. Why did people feel the need to tell you the minutiae of their daily lives? What earthly interest could it be to anyone but themselves unless they wanted to prove something? One day when a friend had posted 'Isn't life great?' Ann hadn't been able to resist responding and had written 'Bully for you!' underneath. The friend had promptly unfriended her from her page.

Ann was used to unusual images being flashed up but this was something else. The face was haggard and world-weary, with eyes that looked as if the soul had gone out of them. It was like something out of a horror movie only this was a real person. That made it worse. It was the face of someone who had been languishing in jail for years. He had committed some horrendous crime or other. She couldn't recall what. Murder, possibly.

Ann only used the site for professional purposes like when she wanted to let people know about a great new art show or to advertise her work. It was a pity not to make use of any media outlet you could lay your hands on. God knows it was hard enough getting yourself noticed in the competitive world of art. She had chosen the career much against her parents' wishes, who considered the pursuit a foolhardy occupation, likely to lead nowhere but poverty and destitution and were constantly nagging her to get a proper job. She had been determined to prove them wrong and had embarked on a career as a portrait artist. At least it paid the bills.

Ann painted in the classical tradition and had built up a reasonably successful career for herself, largely through word of mouth. She would ask people to send in photos of themselves rather than ask them to sit for her. It was less time-consuming. Over the years she had learnt that people could only take so much truth about themselves and was wont to embellish, always veering on the side of flattery. She would gloss over any irregular features such a bump in the nose, a spot on the chin, a frown or an unfortunate hairstyle. Consequently she never got complaints and people recommended her to friends.

The caption under the face mentioned that he was a public figure. She seemed to recall that he had been successful in the music business once. The person who had got hold of that photo, whether policeman, prison officer or simply member of the public must have thought they were performing a public service. It would serve as a salutary warning to anyone thinking of entering into a life of crime. The man was a shadow of his former self. He was barely recognisable.

Ann couldn't help studying the face. It was rare that you got the opportunity to observe the consequences of crime on a person, or the effects of a jail sentence. Most people managed to keep a low profile in such circumstances. So that was what jail did to a person. He didn't look like a murderer but then who does? She seemed to recall that he had murdered his wife. She was sure she could see shame in his face.

The face became imprinted on her mind. There was only one thing to do. In order to exorcise it, she would have to paint it. She had never painted a murderer before, at least not to her knowledge. When you thought about it, there must be loads of them just walking around, judging by the number of cases of domestic violence you read about in the papers. Two a day, she remembered. Not all of them got caught and many had their sentences halved for good conduct.

Ann had been looking for a new subject for some time. This would be a new departure. It was someone she would portray just as he was. It wouldn't need embellishments. It would be a challenge, worth spending time on. If the painting was good enough, she might even enter it for the Summer Exhibition at the Royal Academy. That was something she had always aspired to.

Ann spent the rest of the week working on the face. As she painted away, she couldn't help thinking about the crime. The man was artistic. He would have had a sensitive nature. He must have loved his wife. Otherwise he wouldn't have married her. So why had he killed her?

Maybe his wife was young and beautiful and he had come home one day to find her in a compromising position with another man. In a fit of rage and jealousy he had grabbed a knife and driven it into her, thereby sealing his fate. We all had fatal flaws and jealousy was his. His problem was he hadn't been able to control himself. The man had committed an evil act. There was no getting away from that. But the woman had also played her part. She had betrayed him and thereby killed his feelings for her.

The painting was taking longer than she had anticipated. It was hard getting a true likeness. She wanted to portray it all – the anger and the jealousy but also the sadness, the loss and the shame. Weeks turned to months. There was always something not quite right. It needed an extra touch here, a brushstroke there. And every time she looked at the photo, she saw something else. The face was taking over her life. It haunted her during her waking hours and was there in her dreams. If only she could get the thing done, she could be free of it. She needed to get the face out of her mind and onto the canvas.

Finally Ann could do no more. She carefully wrapped up the painting and sent it off by express post to the Summer Exhibition. She had only just managed to get it done before the deadline. She had plenty to keep her occupied. The daily chores had been piling up and there was a backlog of bills to be paid. She decided to give Facebook a wide berth for a while.

Eventually when she was ready to face the barrage of daily details, she logged on again. To her horror the first thing that loomed out at her was the face, or rather her portrait of it. Her painting had been accepted for the Summer Exhibition. One of her friends had kindly taken a photo of it and posted it on their page and it had gone viral.

About the Author
Jenny Palmer returned to her native Lancashire in 2008. In 2012 she published her childhood memoir called Nowhere Better than Home about growing up in rural Lancashire in the 1950s and 60s. She continues to write short stories, poems and articles on local history.

Filling the Space
Helen Laycock

Aqua Libra

It was the red hat that gave him away. I would have recognised it anywhere. He had his back to me, but I knew it was him standing there, fishing, near the bridge. Fishing had been his life.

I recollected his smile… those dimples, those twinkling eyes. Now that I'd found him, I knew I just couldn't leave.

I straddled the fence of number forty-seven and scooped him up in my arms.

'Time to come home, Norris,' I whispered, kicking the head off one of hers as I leapt over the fishpond with the gnome she had stolen from me.

About the Author
Helen Laycock has written eight children's mystery/adventure books, a couple of poetry books and three collections of short stories for adults, one of which includes flash fiction. She has had around thirty wins/shortlistings for poetry and short stories, successes including Words With Jam, The Ryedale Book Festival, *Writing Magazine*, *Writers' News*, *Writers' Forum*, Flash500, Thynks Publications, Erewash Writers and various online contests. She has a story published in *An Earthless Melting Pot* (Quinn Pub.), four pieces in the *One Word Anthology* by Talkback Writers (Alfie Dog Pub.), several entries in *The Aspiring Writers 2013 Winners Anthology* (Blue Dragon Press) and a poem in *Songs of Angels* (Thynks Pub.). She is a regular

contributor to 100-worders on the CaféLit website and is featured in *The Best of CaféLit 2013.*

Hot Chocolate Day

Vanessa Horn

with sprinkles?

I think it was Forrest Gump who said: 'Life is like a box of chocolates.' If so, I think he was right – almost. I'd just change it slightly – not much – to 'Life is like a mug of hot chocolate' and then it would be perfect. Just perfect. I'll tell you why.

March 9th. A new day; cloudless sky of solid blue with a hint of ceramic shine. Just the shade of my best mug, I realise. I've had this for years – won it, in fact, for my 'Springtime' poem at school, aeons ago. So it's special to me, not least because I haven't won anything since. Anyway, as I retrieve my esteemed trophy from the shelf, I'm amazed at the perfect colour match; even the best artist would've been hard pushed to recreate the shade as precisely as this. A coincidence? No – it can't be.

I pause, hovering over the kettle, undecided at first. I don't think I'll use instant chocolate powder – not today. This isn't a usual day; it is going to be poignant – I know that for sure – but, as yet, I'm not sure exactly how it will play out. Dark, light or mixed emotion? I won't find out just yet – maybe in half an hour or so. But as it's unquestionably a day which will warrant recognition, I'll respect it by making it one of those rare occurrences – a special hot chocolate day. Yes. So, ignoring the kettle, I instead begin to gather my ingredients from cupboards and fridge…

Bittersweet chocolate. Just right for the sensations shadowing me since I woke this morning, knowing that today is the day we will find out the results. Make or break. I shave off a generous amount from the bar, immediately releasing its distinctive aroma. Closing my eyes I inhale it like a bee immersing itself in nectar. Bliss! Unable to resist, I treat myself in nibbling a little, savouring the sweetness that contains a tiny hint of… chilli? Similar to the doctor's words turning round to taunt us when we'd been lulled into a sense of false security. Unexpected. Unwelcome. My breath catches and I tell myself to relax. We don't know anything yet. Okay. I select a sharp knife from the drawer and begin to chop the chocolate even more finely on my old wooden board. The repetitive movement provides a welcome diversion. Chopping, chopping. After a few minutes I have a large heap of chocolate shavings ready, plus a little pile put aside for later.

Cream and sugar. I ignore the high-tech mixer which sits smugly in the corner and instead use a wooden spoon to whip these together in my large and slightly cracked ceramic bowl. I enjoy the physical energy that I need to form the stiff peaks in the mixture. Peaks… Troughs. I like these words; they fit nicely into my beating rhythm: peaks and troughs, peaks and troughs. I'm exorcising my worries as I blend and then blend some more: sugar and cream, peaks and troughs. Finishing, I stand back slightly and admire the results which stand to attention in perfectly-whipped glory. A positive sign? I hope so.

Milk. Plain but necessary to the mixture – an essential part, even. It's a basic element – bland, some would say; you might not always notice it's there but you definitely need it; without it, life would be too rich and probably give you a tummy ache. Like the voice of common sense that stops birds from flying too close to the sun or fish from diving too deeply down into the ocean – it keeps life at a sort of a midway point. The milk blends in modestly, fraternising with the cream, sugar and grated chocolate. A dense texture.

Now it's getting to the tricky part; I need to keep the consistency smooth and creamy, simmering it to the exact point where the chocolate melts and marbles into the mixture before blending. I hold my breath as I do this because sometimes the concoction boils and spoils when it approaches this point. It's important – really important – that this doesn't happen today. It's a superstitious thing, really, thinking that however this turns out might somehow affect what happens today. Silly, I know, but everyone has their own idiosyncrasies and quirks and I'm no exception. Thankfully, though, the ingredients combine successfully and I sigh in relief.

Vanilla and cinnamon: the final few touches. A drop of vanilla essence and a tiny pinch of powdered cinnamon to spike up the flavouring. Not entirely necessary but definitely something that enhances, in a *sharp-intake-of-breath* kind of way. Possibly a reminder that you sometimes need a nudge of anxiety to encourage you to appreciate the everyday things – or people – that you may take for granted? I think about this. It wouldn't have to be too much of a nudge, though; just a hint every now and again is quite sufficient. I carefully pour the thick mixture into my sky-blue mug, and then take one more quick peek outside to check that the colours still match. They do.

Whipped cream and sprinkles. Essential or an indulgence? I don't expect I really need to ask that question; I suppose, if you had the choice, you'd always go for the embellishments – the little extra-special finishing touches – if you could. Wouldn't you? After all, they are the things you look most forward to; the little distractions from the everyday, if you like. I watch as the tiny sprinkles begin to penetrate the generous cream topping, sinking happily into its frothiness and creating minute dents as they disappear, never to be seen again…

My mobile jigs a little on the counter beside me and then bursts into full song, abruptly breaking my reverie. I snatch it up, feeling my heart begin to pound painfully in anticipation. It's time – time to face reality.

'Mum? What did they s– Yeah… yeah… all clear? Oh, thank God!' Thankful and grateful, I allow her familiar voice continue to reassure me as I pick up the mug with my free hand and take the first sip of my exquisite drink. Never before has my hot chocolate tasted quite so good.

About the Author
Vanessa Horn is a Junior School teacher who first became interested in writing a few years ago when she took a sabbatical year. Since then, she has written several hundred stories, some of which have been published in magazines, and others having won prizes in short story competitions. She enjoys reading, shopping and going out for meals.

Slippery Slope

Penny Rogers

Pepsi

Today
The first bus leaves at 06.50. I'll be on it.

Day before yesterday
Pack a bag and hide it on top of the cupboard. Just the essentials: change of underwear, warm top, socks, a towel, tissues, make-up, deodorant, toothbrush, toothpaste and Ted.

Yesterday
Have a shower; not enough time in the morning. It won't be difficult to get out of the house without them knowing. They sleep like logs.

Today
Don't look at anyone, must not be recognised.

Day before yesterday
Check connections. I'll have about 40 mins to wait in Randlesford.

Today
Mustn't leave any trace I was here. Don't get a drink. Waste of money and someone might

remember. The coach is late and crowded. I recognise a face about half way down. Don't make eye contact

14.55 Arrive Victoria. They'll be looking for me now, and realise that I deliberately left my phone behind. Feeling lonely and risk buying a cup of tea and a sandwich. The surly woman who serves me hardly glances away from her magazine. Good.

17.00 I wonder if they are worried.

17.15 Man asks me to talk to him. Creep.

Last week
Row with parents. I do go: sometimes.

Day before yesterday
My tutor says he's done all he can and I failed because I didn't do the work.

Today
Find hostel. Room £12.00. Burger and chips £4.50. Coke £1.20. Reassure Ted.

Tomorrow
Meet Delvina, she says she can find me work. Go with her to Lolo's.

About the Author
Penny Rogers writes short stories and flash fiction. She was shortlisted for the Bridport Prize for flash fiction in 2013, has been placed in the Henshaw creative writing

competition and has had stories published in *Writers' Forum*, *Paragraph Planet* and *Bare Fiction*.

MONG

Neil Campbell

J.W. Lees bitter

After my PhD it didn't work out.

I had to look for jobs in colleges. I took some agency work as a note taker at a place in Rochdale, taking notes for a young deaf girl called Emma. I hadn't been in a college environment for years.

The morning passed without incident, and I went out through the barriers to enjoy the spring sunshine and pick up some lunch. I sat on a bench beneath the neo gothic splendour of the town hall, eating the two pies I'd bought from Gregg's and washing them down with a large tea. As I'd walked through the town centre I had seen dozens of young girls pushing prams. There seemed to be a childbirth epidemic in the town.

The kids in the class were being prepared for the workplace, picking up literacy skills they'd missed out on at school. They were being prepared as good citizens; good, conforming citizens. The trouble was there was too much life in some of them for that.

I made notes on the support worker laptop but was dismayed by the teaching standards, especially since I would have killed for such a job myself.

In one of the classes the lecturer set a group

exercise based on the question, *'why do you think they have built the new hospital in the town centre?'* The lecturer then gave them twenty minutes to work on it. After half an hour the lecturer was still looking at her phone. The kids had stopped talking about the hospital long ago, and many of them were also on their phones.

Finally the lecturer asked them to give feedback on the group exercise. There was a young girl from Rossendale, and she had an endearingly broad Lancashire accent. I had chatted to her briefly, and had overheard her talking all morning. She was about five feet tall and worked behind a bar. She was eighteen but looked closer to twelve. When she spoke you immediately realized she was eighteen after all. 'We don't know. Nobody knows,' she said.

Why don't you know? I've given you twenty minutes. At least twenty minutes.'

'The note taker doesn't even know,' she said, pointing at me.

'I'm not allowed to join in. It is not my job.'

'You mong,' she said. At this point the kids burst out laughing but the lecturer looked seriously alarmed.

'No, no, no,' said the Rossendale girl. 'I don't mean mong in the way you mean it. Not the old way. It is a Rochdale thing.'

'That is not an acceptable word,' said the

lecturer, animated – but too late. 'We don't use words like that.'

'Okay but it weren't meant in the way you thought.'

'Any more feedback then on the group task? Why do we think the new hospital has been built in the town centre?'

'I bet you don't even know, Miss.'

I was getting bored, and though I shouldn't have, I piped in with 'She wouldn't set an exercise or ask a question if she didn't know the answer.' I wasn't being sarcastic, although that is a significant element of my personality.

'I thought you said you weren't allowed to join in,' said the Rossendale girl.

'Don't be a mong,' I said. And all the kids laughed, and it was meant as a joke. I was just so bored. I'd been a naughty kid at school, and even though that was many years before the classroom setting seemed to make me revert to type. The rest of the lesson passed without incident, and the lecturer didn't actually give an answer for why the new hospital had been built in the town centre. I smiled to her on the way out, as a way to say sorry for adding to the disruption.

But when I got back on the tram I felt a bit sad for those kids. They were being short changed in that college. In that class anyway. The kids had no motivation and the lecturer seemed to get away with being shit. Nobody complains about the lecturer at that age or in that environment. The kids don't really know that they can.

The next morning I got on the tram heading back to Rochdale. There was still a week left on the temporary contract and I really needed the money. I was on the tram for ages. I forget exactly where it was, but there was a stretch of the tram line that ran through marshland between low hills. More than once I'd seen the flashing brown of a kestrel in the skies there, and now I spotted it perched on a wire.

I got off the tram and walked past the town hall on my way to the campus. I let myself into the building with my swipe card. As I went to the student support office to pick up the laptop the staff in there didn't seem as friendly as they had been. Then I had a call on my phone.

'Hello?' I said.

'I need you to leave the campus right now.'

'I'm sorry?'

'I need you to leave the campus right now.'

'Why? Who is this?'

'It is Veronica from Hunt Education.'

'But I'm here. I've just come an hour on the tram. What is this about?'

Just then Emma appeared outside. I didn't know sign language so I did my best to communicate to her. She seemed lost. Instead of integrating with the rest of the class I had noticed that she sat on her own at break times, and between classes would always wait around outside the student support office. There was normally an interpreter around who would walk with her to class, but she travelled from the Wirral and hadn't arrived yet.

'Veronica, I've got the student here in front of me.'

I need you to leave the campus.'

'But why?'

'I'm not prepared to discuss this over the phone.'

I felt sick to the stomach. Surely there had been some mistake? I tried as best as I could to explain to Emma that I had to leave, then thankfully her interpreter came. I put the laptop back in the locker in the support office. I am a child of the 70s. A City fan with three master's degrees. The tram had reached Piccadilly before I finally admitted to myself that I've never been good with people.

About the Author
http://www.knivesforksandspoonspress.co.uk/ekphrasis.html

http://www.amazon.co.uk/Hooks-Modern-Dreams-Neil-Campbell-ebook/dp/B00JNYIVDM

Follow on Twitter @neilcambers

Perseverance
Paul Westgate

A glass of dandelion and burdock

The clock's faces showed different times. Instead of a watch my fingers found only the pawn ticket; but what did it matter if I caught the train or not?

She hadn't said no; only that it couldn't work, it would be too difficult. Without speaking she'd looked intently at me, her pale face surrounded by dark fur. I'd said nothing and she'd turned and left the station.

Through clouds of steam I glimpsed the engine's name – 'Perseverance'. I turned around. I now knew what that last look had meant. Gripping the small box tightly, I started walking towards the exit.

About the author
Paul is an enthusiastic but sporadic writer. He lives in Essex and works in London and uses the two train journeys each day to read books, sleep and, occasionally, to think up stories; sometimes these are even written.

Bad

Mary Bevan

Campari soda

'It's awesome, Mum – honestly. When you're in freefall it's like flying, and then the chute opens and suddenly you're rising again like... like the sky's drawing you up. If you knew how it felt you'd want me to do it.'

He looks at me, frowning, willing me to understand. I love him. The fear is all mine, not his.

'OK then, Tom.'

'Yesss.' He springs up from the bench. 'Mum, you're bad!'

Oh, this upside-down language!

I come here most days. The metal plaque on the bench back reads:

> **Thomas Morrison, died 15 March 2014**
> **Why fall?**
> **Skies call.**
> **That's all.**

About the Author
Having promised herself that she'd start writing when she finally gave up work (never too late to learn!), Mary began experimenting with short stories and flash fiction around two years ago. She is particularly fascinated by the exacting demands of the flash fiction form and has won several prizes for her work in literary competitions and story slams.

Shark Bait
Susan A Eames
Cup of hot sweet Rooibos Tea

The cage looks puny.

'You've got to be kidding,' I say.

'It's OK, they never attack the cage,' says Frankie.

'Never?'

'They're not interested in canned diver.'

The little boat smacks into the trough of every oncoming wave while we manoeuvre into position halfway between the mainland and Dyer Island in what is nicknamed, Shark Alley.

Frankie cuts the engine but we continue to buck and bounce in sea-sickening lurches.

The boys get busy chumming the water with putrefying fish. Frankie tosses in a tuna head attached to a buoyed line.

They lower the cage into the water while I wriggle into my thick wetsuit.

Within minutes an immense shadowy figure begins to circle the boat.

Once, twice. On its third circuit, the shark lunges for the bait which Frankie twitches aside to encourage it to stay and fight for its meal. Instead the animal spooks and vanishes.

Another Great White torpedoes in. Three metres of menace just off our stern churns the water into foam as it grabs and tries to detach the tuna from the line. The shark gives up and zig-zags away.

The top of the cage rides above the waterline. 'Get in,' says Frankie.

I hesitate.

'What are you waiting for? C'mon!'

I plop into the bobbing cage. Icy cold waves slap the back of my head.

We wait.

Before long another Great White rockets in.

'Dive down!' yells Frankie.

I gulp a breath and sink underwater. Stunning silence. Unthinking, I hook my toes through one of the cage bars for balance. Eyes wide behind my mask, I look around. Where?

Then the sun pierces the gloom. Backlit in a dazzling illumination, the shimmering shark slices, skims and skews towards me.

Jesusmaryandjoseph

With a spurt of alarm, I yank my toes back inside the cage.

Up above Frankie jerks the tuna head and the shark slews past the cage like it's attached to the line.

And it's so stupendously, unexpectedly beautiful, I am without fear.

About the Author
Susan A. Eames left England over twenty five years ago to explore the world and dive its oceans. She has had travel articles and short fiction published on three continents.

After several fascinating years living in Fiji she has relocated to West Cork in Ireland.

Jigsaw
Debz Hobbs-Wyatt

A glass of milk and a cookie

It's a chronological disorder. People call it different things. I call it *travelling*.

I don't know when it's gonna happen, usually starts with the smell of burning; which is weird, given what happened.

Nan left the gas on.

Mum forgot the batteries for the smoke detector.

Dad died.

I found a pierce of the jigsaw, the one we were doing. 'It's getting late,' Dad said. 'We'll finish it tomorrow.'

But there was no tomorrow.

Now I'm gonna put it right.

Gonna find a way to *travel*.

I'll warn Nan. Tell Mum about the batteries.

I'll finish the jigsaw with Dad.

About the Author
Debz edits for CaféLit, is an award winning short story writer, published novelist... hey too egotistical? Forget that. Debz writes because she cannot **no**t write, she also works, to pay the bills, as an editor and professional critter (critiques not fully animals)... no forget that too. Let's just say: this is a 100 word version of the first story she ever had published in a collection (2008) and might

inspire some of you to do the same thing and adapt a story you already have! And if she adds these fifteen words her bio will also be exactly 100 words.

Head Banging

Sue Cross

G and T

I had just returned from a visit to the supermarket when the phone rang.

'Pamela! What a surprise – how are you?' I uttered before I could bite my tongue in regret.

'I've had an awful few months. The migraines are forever lurking behind my eyes,' she moaned.

I sat down, knowing that this would be a long conversation. After commiserating, she asked if we could meet for lunch.

'Are you sure that you'll be up to it. You know, the migraines…'

'I must make the effort. I've not been out for ages. Shall we meet at the Wine Bar in Grove Road?'

It was arranged and we met on the dot at twelve noon. Pamela had lost weight since I had last seen her and she looked pale. In spite of the heat she wore a beige body warmer over her pristine, white blouse. Although she could be irritating, I was fond of her and I felt sorry that she had to suffer such poor health. We pecked each other on the cheek and I hoped that my perfume would not cause an allergic reaction. Silly of me to have put it on, but it was habit.

We found a quiet table in the window and soon

the waiter greeted us. He had docile eyes and sported a tattoo of a spider's web on his neck.

'The special today is Chicken Chasseur with new potatoes and either salad or green beans.'

Pamela screwed her nose up and perused the menu.

'Shall I come back?' he asked.

'Er, yes. This table is no good. The sun will be round in a minute. Can we sit in the shade? Migraines.' She sounded ominous and the waiter's eyebrows raised a fraction.

We duly found a table near to the kitchen, where it was suitably gloomy, and ordered some drinks.

'White wine for me, please. What would you like, Pamela?'

'Er, let me think. Mineral water, still. Thank you.'

The waiter returned with our drinks and asked if we were ready to order.

'I'll have the special, please – with the green beans.'

He scribbled in his notepad and looked expectantly at Pamela, who was wearing a pained expression. I hoped that it was not the start of a migraine.

'Er, let me think. I'll have the pâté with white bread. No butter. Dairy allergy. Does the pâté contain any dairy?'

'I'll check for you.' He smiled and disappeared. My tummy rumbled.

'Well, this is nice. Cheers.' I raised my glass and took a gulp of wine.

'I've come off the blood pressure pills,' Pamela informed me. 'They were causing so many problems. George has been doing all the housework and cooking. I couldn't get out of bed for a month.'

The waiter returned, looking triumphant. 'No dairy products in the pâté.'

'All right. I'll have that, then.'

He looked relieved and disappeared with haste before she could change her mind.

My mouth watered as the food was presented. It smelled delicious and soon I was tucking into my meal. The chicken was tender and succulent, the sauce rich and the green beans crisp.

Pamela picked at her food and complained about the incompetence of the medical profession.

'Everything all right here?' The waiter held his head to one side, like an expectant sparrow.

'Delicious.' I meant it.

'The bread is a bit doughy and the pâté is too rich. You can take my plate away. I can't finish it.' Pamela adjusted her sunglasses and took some tablets from her handbag.

'Can I get you anything else? Coffee or dessert?'

'Coffee please. What about you, Pamela?'

'Er, let me think. I'll have a chamomile tea.'

I heard a lot about the side effects of modern drugs as we waited for our drinks. It really was a shock to learn of the dangers of such medicines.

After paying our bill, I asked Pamela if she would like a lift home. I was worried that she was too delicate to manage the half-mile walk to her house.

'Thank you, dear. I am rather tired.'

'I'm parked in the car park around the corner.'

'These new bifocals are so difficult to get used to,' she announced as we strolled to the car park but, before I could steady her, she was on the pavement, prone and moaning.

'Are you all right?' I helped her to her feet.

'Banged my head. I'll be fine,' she said with uncharacteristic optimism.

'Are you sure? I can drive you round to A and E.'

'No need to fuss. I'm all right.'

I drove her home and, worried, phoned her the next day.

'How are you feeling today?' I braced myself for a detailed description.

'Oh, fine. It was lovely seeing you yesterday. Can we do it again next week?' She sounded chirpy and cheerful.

We met at the same wine bar. She was a little late and breezed in looking ten years younger. I tried to fathom what was different about her and then realised that she was not wearing her dark glasses and she was wearing eye makeup. Eye makeup! She was allergic to eye makeup and had often described the alarming the effects of even the slightest hint of mascara.

Let's sit in the window. It's such a lovely day.'

'Are you sure?'

'Yes, why do you ask?'

'Oh, you know. Just wondered.'

We had a different waiter this time. 'Can I get you a drink?' he enquired.

'I'd like a gin and tonic. What about you, dear?' Pamela looked at me, smiling.

I ordered my usual glass of Chardonnay.

'The special today is steak in a creamy pepper sauce with chips and side salad or broccoli.'

'Yum – sounds good to me. I'll have mine rare with broccoli,' Pamela enthused.

The waiter disappeared to the kitchen and I sat in silent shock.

'So, how have you been since your fall?'

'Fall, what fall? I don't know – my memory has been shocking this week, but what the heck! Cheers, drink up. I'm going to have another G and T.'

About the Author
Sue Cross has published two novels, *Tea at Sam's* and the sequel, *Making Scents*. You can visit her on her website www.suecross.com

Paris

Roger Noons

A glass of absinthe

When I asked the waitress for a quickie, she slapped my face and flounced off towards the kitchen. Seeing my look of hurt and embarrassment, the man at the next table leaned over and said. 'I think you'll find it's pronounced Quiche.' That summed up my first day in Paris. The second was no better. I slipped on a wet path and fell into the Seine.

They say things come in threes, so I took great care visiting the Musée d'Orsay. Did you by any chance read about an accident in a Paris museum, where a Rodin statue was…

About the Author
Roger is a regular contributor to CaféLit and his work is featured in *The Best of* collections. He charms us all with his humour but sometimes also his pathos.

New Term
Gill James

Black coffee: keep it coming

Greg plugged in his computer and hooked up to the internet. Up against the wall there was a red crate containing Sonia's stuff. Her desk would go there eventually. After having an office to himself for six years he now had to share. Still, this building had more character than the other one and Sonia was hardly ever there.

He clicked on his Virtual Learning Environment. Seminar groups, reading lists and lecture notes were all stored there neatly as you would expect. Teaching would start on Monday.

One day of freedom, then, before the students made him feel inadequate again.

About the Author
Gill James is a Senior Lecturer at the University of Salford where she is Programme Leader for English and Creative Practice. She writes fiction for young adults and children and shorter fiction for adults. Her latest novel is *The House on Schellberg Street*.

@gilljames
www.gilljames.co.uk
http://gilljames.blogspot.co.uk/
http://www.thehouseonschellbergstreet.com/

Never Again!

Janet Bunce

A caffeine shot

There was so much pain in her body she felt like she had moved to old age overnight.
Adrenalin pumping, forcing legs on.
Mentally she was challenged but the 'Can I go on?' was losing out to 'I will go on'.
She had seen some fall by the wayside along the way. Exhaustion, pain or injury taking them.
Her heart went out to these gallant people.
She was touched by all who had come out to offer support.
It brought tears to her eyes.
She turned the final corner and saw it.
The finish line – another 26.2 miles completed!

About the Author
About the author: Janet lives in Epping Forest and works part time in financial services. She has been pleased to have two stories published in the latest edition of the Best of Cafélit. This 100 worder is inspired by her own experiences of running marathons and she is 'looking forward' to running London marathon later this month!

Editor's Note: This story was published on the web site just before Janet competed in this year's London marathon!

Monday Morning
Roger Noons

A large mug of hot chocolate

At the bus stop, in last night's make-up, the woman felt her cheeks warm under the schoolboy's stare. He hitched up his backpack, but his eyes never left her face.

'Are you a clown?'

She started, thought to rebuke him, but instead sneaked a glance at her reflection in the graffitied plastic. When she saw the streaked mascara and scratched foundation, she laughed. 'I wish I was,' she admitted and touched the boy's shoulder, tempted to tousle his hair.

When the bus arrived, she let him get on first. She slipped on her sling backs as he did so.

About the Author
Roger is featured in *The Best of* collections. He charms us all with his humour as well as his pathos.

Josie The Spy
David Deanshaw

Tea turned cold on a window ledge

Josie carefully peeled back the grimy net curtain and stared out of her attic window. She did so because she had noticed that the front door of number 37, across the street, had opened at last. She stood behind the mounted camera, looked through the view finder and clicked three times. The street lights were some distance away so the clandestine activities she had just witnessed were only just visible.

Two men were struggling to carry a long bag wrapped in a dark grey material along the short garden path. Then they dropped it casually into the back of a white van parked on the road outside the house. It must have been really heavy because she heard a dull thud even though her house was thirty metres away.

She reached for the special phone with dithering hands. Nervously she pressed three buttons as she had been instructed. A voice answered with one word – 'Speak.' She did so in hushed tones and reported: 'They are leaving now!' She sat down on the chair nearby and was surprised just how breathless she felt as she put the phone down, so much excitement!

At last she could relax. Her job was done.

It had all been such a surprise. A week earlier, two

men, one very tall, the other sort of average height, both dressed in trench coats had arrived at her door. They showed a form of identification she had not been able to make out fully because she had answered the door wearing her TV glasses. They had introduced themselves as "Special Services" people and asked that they should be invited inside.

'Mrs Parker,' they began, 'we are urgently in need of a location which overlooks the front door of a house opposite. Do you know who lives at number 37? Also, are they friends of yours?'

'Oh no, not friends at all,' she replied with a gasp. 'I think they work shifts, perhaps at the airport because they wear dark blue overalls. They only come home during the night. They're very careful not to slam doors, I must say. But they don't have any milk delivered, or post or papers, for that matter. Sometimes there is a light burning in the cellar, even during the day.'

'Mrs Parker,' the tall one replied, 'I am sure that we have found the right neighbour to carry out a short spying mission for us. Are you willing to have a camera mounted in your attic, with its lens trained on number 37?'

'Oh isn't this exciting. Why do you want to do this?'

'Now Mrs Parker, this is a secret operation and we do not expect you to tell anybody about what you are doing or why we have asked you to carry out this mission for us. Do you understand?'

'Oh I'm sure that I will be able to keep a secret – just for a week is it? OK. So long as I can tell my neighbours afterwards. Everyone at bingo will be really interested.'

'Mrs Parker, the whole nation is relying on you to be helpful to us. When the mission is finished we will then release you from your agreement.'

'What agreement?' she asked with surprise.

'Oh didn't we tell you. We have a document here like the Official Secrets Act which you have to sign. Print your name and then sign on the line below.'

'Will I get paid for this?' Josie's interest was pricked by this thought.

'Oh I'm sure that we could justify something like a week's rent, if you really insist.'

'Oh, I do. Well I pay the Council £300 a week for this small house, so could it be two weeks rent? Please!'

The short one looked up at the tall one, they both nodded and Josie was overjoyed.

'Now tell me exactly what you want me to do.'

'Well it is important that we get pictures of what they are doing. We have had a man in the street for a few days now and he had nothing to report. That may be because they have suspected that they are being watched. This is a simple camera with a special night vision lens. We will set it up on a tripod to keep it steady in your attic. All you have to do is watch for when the door opens, click this button two or three times. Then we want you to use this special mobile phone, press these three buttons which will call us.'

'Are you going to tell me why you are doing this?'

'Not until afterwards, when we come to give you your money, we will tell you what it has all been about. And then you can tell your friends, but not before. Is that alright?'

'And you promise that I can tell all the girls at bingo when it's all over?'

'Yes you can.' The prospects of being the centre of attention at bingo, AND having six hundred pounds in her purse gave her frisson of expectation.

Now one week on from that strange day, she had done everything the two strange men had asked and made the call.

Within just a few minutes she could hear a siren and the street was full of police cars. Number 37 was surrounded, the door was smashed in and later four men wearing dark blue overalls were led out to a police van.

Later, another large police van arrived and several long bags were loaded, all in the same dark grey plastic wrapping.

Josie Parker had played her part in busting a gang of carpet rustlers.

About The Author
David Deanshaw has had a varied business career, initially in banking, then as a management consultant and more recently involved in the regeneration of run down town centres.

He has used his experience in writing a mixture of short stories, whilst planning on writing about situations he saw in the fields of both finance and politics. He has had several letters published in *The Times*, *Sunday Times* and *Birmingham Post* of a political and business nature.

His first novel, *The Price of Loyalty*, is based on the greed, ambition and arrogance he found watching activity in the City of London, entwined with political machinations. A sequel is being written together with a prequel involving some of the older characters.

Web-based Artist
Mike Olley

Shoo-Fly Punch

A spider has taken over our shed down the bottom of the garden. We can't use it any more. People say we're silly to be scared of spiders but this one shouts and swears if we approach him, let alone suggest it should leave.

'I'm an artist,' he says. 'Away, philistines! I'm creating.'

He uses our tools and doesn't contribute to the rent. Sometimes he works throughout the night, making noise and mess. The neighbours complained but there's nothing we can do, genius is not nine-to-five.

So, the landlord is evicting us. Well, good luck with telling the spider.

About the author
Mike Olley made music videos but gave it all up to live next to a Spanish castle, where he grew cactuses, practised carpentry and wrote strange funny stories. A quirk of fate brought him to the English seaside where he continues to write. Published in several anthologies, his own collection of short stories is entitled *Better*. Mikeolley.com

Dialling 999
Vicky Jacobson
Black Coffee

Generally, if things go wrong, my first reaction is to panic – okay, you might not see me running round flapping my arms like the proverbial headless chicken, but believe me, that's what's going on inside and that's what was happening last night when I had to call 999.

I couldn't find my phone, I couldn't find my phone – my hands were shaking as I searched my bag but – no, I really couldn't find my phone. I scrabbled frantically through dozens of old receipts and shopping lists, checked all the pockets, one after another but no sign of it. I prayed that I'd not forgotten it again and tried to calm myself but the panic was rising. I tried once more: I closed my eyes and took a deep breath, held it and concentrated on counting to ten as I slowly let it out. I opened my eyes and started looking again and there it was – in the first bloody place I'd looked. I focused all my attention on hitting the number nine three times and finally, with relief, I heard a calm voice on the other end asking me what service I required.

'Um, um, ambulance, no police – um, ambulance and police,' I managed to blurt, 'there's a man, he's unconscious… he might be dead… oh god, there's blood everywhere.'

The operator asked me where I was and I gave her the town and tried to explain my location – I wasn't exactly sure of an address but I told her it was off the footpath leading from Garrison Road. 'About half-way along there's a gap in the hedge and he's through there, down in the field.' I was sobbing by this time and she spoke soothingly and said somebody would be with me shortly.

Although the path is well-known to locals, it isn't very well lit and runs through an area bounded by fields on one side and waste ground on the other so normally, I wouldn't use it after dark. As usual though, I was running late so the few minutes I knew it would save, swayed me.

I remembered seeing a man coming towards me and as he neared he'd asked for a light and I shook my head and said I didn't smoke. The next thing I knew I was sprawling on the ground down the bank and the man was coming after me. It all got very hazy after that but I recalled a struggle and felt several blows then I had hold of a rock and was swinging it with all the strength I could muster. I can still hear the crunch as the rock made contact with something hard but then it all faded away. The next thing I knew the man was lying still on the ground and I must have gotten to my feet because I was standing up and looking down at him and I knew I needed to get help.

I could still hear the operator speaking but it appeared that she was no longer able to hear me and then the phone went dead in my hand. By that point though I could hear sirens approaching so I tried to make my way back up to the path. A few minutes later I heard the sound of vehicles screeching to a halt and car doors slamming. I saw several figures running towards me holding torches but I was a little bewildered when they totally ignored me and hurried into the field.

I followed them to the gap in the hedge and watched as one of the policemen knelt down and checked the bloke's vital signs. 'It's too late for this one,' he said, 'we'll need to secure the area and get the forensics boys out here.' He stood up and shone his torch around the field stopping at a low heap further off. 'What's that?' he asked and one of the other policemen walked over to where the torch beam was directed.

'Sir, it's a woman and she's in a bad way,' he said, bending down to look at her, then more urgently, 'she's still alive Guv but only just – we need to get the paramedics here pronto.'

A chill ran through me and I slipped back into the shadows beneath the bushes. I couldn't understand what they were saying, there'd only been me and that bloke – where had this other woman come from?

Two guys rushed through the gap and I saw them load the woman onto a stretcher with swift, practised movements. I tried to press back into the hedge to avoid being seen but as they passed me the woman's hand slipped from under the blanket and brushed against my leg. A glint on her wrist resolved itself into a watch that looked very familiar.

A thought, dismissed before it was fully formed, flitted across my mind as I lifted my hand to look at the watch I was wearing.

It was... no, it had to be a coincidence, she was just wearing a watch like mine; but there was the scratch on the glass where I'd caught it on a wall while rushing to get washing in from the rain and there was the tiny splodge of white paint on the strap I'd never gotten round to cleaning off. It wasn't just like mine; it was mine.

In disbelief, I fumbled to look at my own wrist again and, as I did, the truth finally slammed into me. I felt a huge jolt as I was pulled back into my body and then, for a brief moment, I was aware of being carried on the stretcher before everything went black.

I woke up the next day in hospital. The police were waiting to speak to me and I learned that I'd been attacked but evidence showed that I'd fought back desperately. My attacker had suffered a head injury during the tussle and had died and the doctor said that I'd probably be dead too if it hadn't been for the mystery woman who'd used my mobile to summon help. They said that she'd disappeared before the police arrived but they obviously needed to interview her and thought an appeal in the local paper might urge her to come forward. I knew that was very unlikely but thought I should probably keep that to myself.

I can't explain what happened last night but I do know that I'll be sticking to roads with street lights in future.

Yesterday I phoned 999 for the first time. I want it to be the last.

About the Author
Vicky is a retired legal secretary with two grown-up children. She has always had a desire to write but only really got started when she joined Canvey Writers earlier this year. This story was a response to a writing prompt from the group.

For The Love of Harley
Eleanor Patrick

Bucks Fizz

'Don't speak,' said Gran sharply, without turning from the computer screen. 'I'm just about to win us a Harley Davidson.'

Beth stopped mid-sentence and swung round from the ironing board. Gran was hunched over Beth's desk, in front of eBay, a look of fierce concentration on her face.

'Gran, stop!' cried Beth, rushing over and trying to grab the mouse from her grandmother's hand. 'You're only on there to buy a few books. You can't surely need a motorbike at eighty. And anyway, how are you going to pay for it?'

'With your PayPal account, I imagine,' said Gran, sheepishly. 'I haven't got one of my own. And the auction's just ended… See? It's mine! So you'll soon see how I ride. Haven't been on a bike in years.'

Beth leaned over Gran's shoulder and stared from the screen to her grandmother and back, incredulous. 'Gran! A Harley Davidson? Condition, used. Previous owners, two! What are you doing?' She shook her head in mock disbelief. 'I should have kept an eye on you,' she said. 'You're always up to something!'

She straightened up and perched herself on the arm of Gran's chair. Impulsively, she gave the old lady a hug, feeling a surge of affection for her that she certainly didn't deserve at that minute. 'Well... so long as you pay me back...'

Her words were intentionally light, but a seed of worry was germinating at the back of her mind. Not about the money. Gran had loads. But her mother had whispered privately when dropping her off at Beth's house: 'Keep an eye on her, will you? See how she's managing. I'm a little bit worried... at her age, you know...'

Gran usually lived on her own, sixty miles away and Beth knew her mum worried too much about her. Beth knew Gran was fine. But if Gran started doing things that Mum could label 'bizarre', Beth was going to have trouble defending her. She pushed the thought down. This was Gran having fun, as she always had, for as long as Beth could remember.

'Gran! What mad idea will you dream up next?' She stroked her grandmother's cheek, gave her a friendly pat on the arm and stood up. 'Who'd have thought it of you? A motorbike!'

Gran smiled a secretive smile, solemnly clicked out of eBay and shut the computer down. 'You can pay for it later,' she said, standing up and stretching. 'We'll have to go to the bank this afternoon and transfer some money to your account... Do you know? I'm excited. A real Harley Davidson at last!'

Before Beth could ask what she meant by 'at last', the old lady disappeared upstairs so fast that Beth almost imagined a draught. There was nothing wrong with her physically, at least, she reflected ruefully.

'So what is it about the motorbike?' Beth asked casually as they laid the table for lunch together. Sharing leisurely meals with Gran was making this visit a proper treat.

'Oh that. It's a long story,' said Gran, stroking her finger slowly round the edge of a plate.

'Well there's plenty of time before you go home. Mum and Dad aren't back for another three weeks.'

Beth watched expectantly as Gran tore open a roll and stuffed it with cheese. One of her earliest memories was afternoon tea with Gran – filling home-baked rolls with anything they could find in the larder of her old Victorian kitchen.

They'd always been close – more like mother and daughter really – sharing many hours together while her parents had built up their bookshop business. Now, years later, her parents were on a 30th wedding anniversary cruise. With no one living near enough if Gran needed help, Mum had decreed Gran should stay with Beth while they were away. Neither Gran nor Beth had demurred. They were like two schoolgirls in a secret society.

'Madeira, Canaries, Channel Islands…' mused Gran, licking a finger.

'Stop evading the question! Why a motorbike when you said you wanted something new to read at bedtime?'

Gran looked up and grinned. Her lined face was transformed. 'Well since your mum and dad can't hear me, I'll tell you how it happened…

'I was always a bit of a tomboy, you know. Playing down the lane when I was a kid, talking to the men at the garage where my dad – your great grandad – did the accounts. I even went in to help him after school when I was older. Much better than learning how to do housework! And that's where I met Charles, bless his heart. He was always bringing in that old bike of his. The sort with wide handlebars. Took me for a spin in it sometimes. I guess that's when I lost my heart. He was so…'

Gran paused, as if unable to find just the right word. Beth suspected she was remembering him, the wind in his hair, the grin on his face, the noise of the bike and the feel of being a passenger on the back. 'Sexy' was the word that came to mind.

'He was what they call… a smasher?' she ventured, erring on the side of wisdom. 'I do wish I'd met him. He must have been okay if he liked you!'

'Oh Beth, you always know how to say the right thing! Pour me another cup, would you?'

Beth obliged. 'So you married him?' she prompted.

'Oh yes. But it caused a furore of the first order!' said Gran, gesturing with her arms to show the size of the trouble she'd caused. 'How dare I marry someone who went around on one of those things? What was I thinking of?'

She frowned. 'They were a bit straight-laced, you know. Wanted me to marry a professor or something equally boring. Hah! The thought of it. Where's the adventure in a musty old university room, I ask you?'

Beth smiled. They talked on about Gran's childhood, making third and fourth cups of tea as the sun moved round the sky, sending a sharp burst of light into Beth's little kitchen-diner. The setting might be different but it felt as if she were young again, enthralled by Gran's never-ending fund of stories, hoping the day would never end, and that her parents would not come to pick her up.

When they strolled down to the shops, enjoying the cool breeze that had blown up, Beth was pleased to see how well Gran was walking – two miles every day, she claimed, at eighty. Beth hoped she'd be able to do the same at that age. But ride a Harley Davidson? She didn't think so. And some people, she reflected soberly, might even think it wasn't quite normal to want to. But she simply couldn't accept that Gran was anything other than in her right mind – that sort of thing happened to other grans, not hers.

Outside the bank, they paused to admire the council's flower tubs, cascading with geraniums and busy lizzies.

'We always used to have flowers around when Charles was alive,' Gran said wistfully. 'He wasn't just a motorbike man, you know. He liked living things, too. Mind you, you'd have thought that bike of his was alive, the way he tended it!'

'You still haven't told me why the Harley Davidson in particular, Gran,' Beth said. It was like pulling teeth. But she needed an answer to assuage her doubts. 'Dad always said you were dark, difficult and dangerous. I'm beginning to agree with him,' she teased.

'It was his heart's desire,' said Gran, simply. 'He saved up for one from the day we married. Worked down at the picture house in town. Didn't get much pay, and then your mother came along and we had nothing to spare. But he still dreamed of owning one.'

She bent to one of the flowers and took a long moment savouring its smell. When she continued, her voice was stronger. 'We can all dream. Sometimes you get what you dream of, sometimes you don't. But Charles was cheated. He got lung trouble and had to give up riding. Couldn't even manage the small bike he had—

'Oh don't feel sad,' she said quickly as Beth opened her mouth to speak. 'We had several more years and great fun. But the thing was, he never got the bike. Never got the Harley Davidson. And something's been unfinished all these years. Well, now I've done it for him!'

Again, Beth felt a stirring of disquiet, much as she was devoted to Gran. But all she said was 'Well, let's get on and go home and pay for it, then. Usually people arrange delivery as soon as they get the money. But I've no idea how they transport bikes!'

She couldn't make herself ask what she was thinking, which was: what was Gran going to *do* with it? She shook her head as they went into the bank.

That night, Beth fell asleep worrying about the promised arrival of the bike in two days' time. The owner, going by the name of 'grimlad26', was using a trailer firm to send it down from York. After they'd settled it by email, Gran had seemed strangely contented all evening, quietly turning the pages of a magazine, eating chocolates and humming a little to herself. *Stop worrying*, Beth told herself. But she was anxious and restless. As if she'd colluded with a fantasy.

When Thursday came, Gran and Beth waited, one excitedly, the other anxiously, for the promised trailer to arrive, bearing the 'chopper/cruiser with lots of customised features and only 1875 miles on the clock' – according to the auction details that Beth had read over and over in the intervening day. Gran seemed completely unfazed about becoming the owner of such a machine.

Teatime approached and they stood together at the chopping board in the kitchen preparing vegetables for the evening meal, hardly talking.

As the clock struck six, Beth's anxiety turned to frustration. 'I don't think it's coming,' she said flatly, slamming the lid on the pan with the broccoli. 'I think we've been conned. The man definitely said Thursday and Thursday is nearly over. Delivery firms don't work this late.'

'Conned?' said Gran, looking up from slicing the carrots. 'Of course not. We'd give him bad feedback. And why would a Harley Davidson owner con us? They're not like that.'

'People are like all sorts of things these days,' said Beth, her cross mood evaporating to sadness. 'I think—'

A sudden noise penetrated the walls of the kitchen. They froze and listened. Unmistakeably, an engine was roaring up the street, louder and louder until it could only be right outside. Then the sound cut dead.

Beth stared at Gran in the silence. '…we should go and see,' she finished. Her mouth was nearly too dry to swallow.

Beth nudged protectively in front of Gran as they raced down the hall. Pulling open the door, they were faced with a swathe of shiny black leather and a space-like helmet in pristine gold and black. Beth felt Gran shiver as they stood side by side staring open-mouthed at the man on the step. He was probably middle-aged, though it was difficult to tell under all the gear.

'Grimlad26,' he said from inside the helmet in a warm, friendly voice to Beth. 'Are you Mrs Bickley?'

'*This* is Mrs Bickley,' said Beth indicating Gran. The slightest flicker of something Beth couldn't read crossed Grimlad's face.

But Gran's eyes were on the gleaming machine at the gate – a vision in chrome at the front, middle and back. 'What happened to the trailer?' she asked. 'Well, never mind, you're here now. I knew you'd come. But you were very late,' she accused, lifting her lined face and glaring fiercely at him.

'Trouble with the firm, Mrs Bickley,' said Grimlad cheerfully. 'So I decided to ride her down. Took a bit longer than the trailer job would have. And added three hundred miles to the clock, unfortunately. But she went like a dream. Forgotten how much fun she was. Work takes all my free time these days,' he added regretfully.

Gran walked out on the pavement. 'The keys?' she asked, in a dreamy sort of voice.

'Madam, you need a license to drive one of these! I assumed it was for your son or daughter.'

'It was for my husband Charles, actually,' said Gran. 'Deceased.' Her shoulders slumped. 'And you're right. I don't have a licence. I got carried away.'

Beth saw the rapture drain from Gran's face and an intense sadness flood into it as she walked round the Harley Davidson, stroking the leather seat reverentially and inspecting the gleaming bodywork.

Beth looked at Grimlad and raised her eyebrows, grimacing in resignation. She had no idea how to handle this situation. It was getting rapidly out of hand. But Grimlad looked her directly in the eye, seemed to understand something he read there, and slowly nodded his head.

'Mrs Bickley, I have a suggestion, if I may?' he said, addressing Gran's back.

Gran turned to look at him. Beth's heart lurched to see her face. She should have stopped this 'bit of fun' before it started.

Grimlad unlocked the bootbox. 'There's a spare crash helmet in here. Would you... sorry... May I have the pleasure of giving you a spin on the old machine, M'Lady? It would be a privilege.'

For a moment no one moved. Then Gran's lips turned up slightly at the edges and a grin of anticipation spread over her face. 'Would you? That would be... I mean, thank you kindly, gracious sir.'

She made him a tiny curtsy.

Beth felt as if she'd been dropped into the set of a television costume drama, except that no one in *Pride and Prejudice* wore leathers and a crash helmet, and Gran still had her apron on.

Three times Gran and Grimlad26 raced round the estate on the Harley Davidson, while Beth leaned limply against the fence hoping against hope that the neighbours were watching their televisions. Grimlad, however, seemed perfectly happy, and afterwards, Gran, flushed and proud, invited him in. 'You've driven miles today. Let me offer you some refreshment.'

Grimlad hooked his helmet over the knob at the bottom of the bannister and stripped off his leather jacket. He took the lemonade that Beth passed him.

'Too hot for riding really,' he said as he drained the last drop. 'But if Gran would like one more spin…?'

'Gran would not,' said Gran. 'Thanks, but I'd forgotten how uncomfortable it is to be astride a great horse of a machine. I must have been too entranced by Charles to mind!' She paused. 'I bought it to honour Charles' memory, to finish the story, so to speak. I'm not sure what happens next.'

A stunned silence greeted this announcement. Beth's heart sank. This was one step short of crazy.

How was she going to explain a redundant Harley Davidson to her mother?

'I'm getting old,' said Gran sadly, as they sat down to their much delayed meal. 'Not making decisions like I used to. Must be something wrong with me to get such ideas in my head.' She toyed with her broccoli, wiping it through the tomato sauce before lifting it slowly to her mouth.

'There's nothing at all wrong with you, Gran! Nothing at all,' Beth repeated firmly, knowing it now to be true. 'That was the perfect thing to have done for Charles. And the perfect follow-up.'

Gran looked up. 'You know something? He sounded so like Charles when he spoke of his love for the bike that I couldn't refuse to let him buy it back. I'd have had to be heartless.'

Beth smiled. Her ears were still ringing gratefully from the sound of Grimlad26 roaring off, to the motorway and on to York. 'It reminded me of when I was a kid at your house,' she said to Gran, picking her words carefully, 'when we did all sorts of things we never told my parents about. Our secret adventures, you called them.'

Gran looked up thoughtfully. 'You're right,' she said, after a pause in which Beth held her breath. 'Some things are much better if they're kept quiet.'

Giving Beth a conspiratorial wink, she waded into her meal with relish.

About the Author
Eleanor is a freelance writer, editor and proofreader. She has published three books for younger people and is currently studying illustration. You can commission her at www.eleanorpatrick.co.uk or read her blog at http://eleanorpatrick.wordpress.com or even follow her on Twitter @EleanorMPatrick. She'd love to connect!

Sex and Socks and Rock 'n' Roll
Susan A. Eames

Glass of chilled Singha Beer

'You want see Ping Pong Show?'
'Good grief, no.'
Maud hurried to find Alfie. He was rummaging through packs of socks on a market stall. In the notorious Patpong area of Bangkok, surrounded by Go-go Bars featuring skinny girls in white bikinis gyrating to rock music, Alfie had nevertheless been distracted by socks.
'Look at these, Maud. Five pairs for the equivalent of a quid. Do you think I should buy some?'
'Forget the socks, it's time to go. I've just been propositioned.'
'Really? Do you want me to thump him?'
'It was a "she".'
'Really? How... interesting. Was she, um... pretty?'
'You're disgusting sometimes.'
'Maybe she was a lady boy?'
'Hardly. She was a middle aged, bandy-legged crone, and she asked me if I wanted to see a Ping Pong show.'
'And... do you?'
'For heaven's sake, Alfie. Why would I want to see girls doing unnatural things with ping pong balls?'

'Well, you know. Just out of curiosity. We said we'd explore the local culture after all.'

'Don't be absurd. That isn't culture.' Maud fixed Alfie with a hard stare. 'You want to go, don't you?'

'Maudie, Maudie, I'd say you are just as inquisitive as me. And you'd have quite a story to tell when we get home.'

'Good grief, I wouldn't tell anyone.'

'What happens in Bangkok, stays in Bangkok?'

'Whatever would people think of us?'

'OK, we won't tell your friends at the gardening club. Where's the show?'

'Slow down, Tiger, I haven't agreed to anything.'

'Come on, Maudie-kins. Admit it. A little bit of titillation never hurt anyone.'

Maud frowned. 'We're too old for this lark, Alfie.'

'No, I won't accept that, Maud. The day we admit we're too old for a bit of slap and tickle is the day we may as well lay down and die.'

Maud looked at Alfie, shocked. Then she unexpectedly laughed. 'All right, let's do it… but you must promise not to tell.'

'Don't fret, old girl, I won't tell a soul.' Alf suppressed an excited giggle. 'Hang on while I buy these socks.'

About the Author
Susan A. Eames left England over twenty five years ago to explore the world and dive its oceans. She has had travel

articles and short fiction published on three continents. After several fascinating years living in Fiji she has relocated to West Cork in Ireland.

Susan blogs at:
http://susan-a-eamestravelfictionandphotos.blogspot.ie

Scarf Girl

Penny Rogers

Tap Water

Once upon a time a little girl called Alina was born in a small town somewhere on the eastern edge of Europe. She had an idyllic childhood, playing with her dolls in the lovely garden around her house and skating on the lake in winter. But all this changed the day her father went to work and didn't come back. When Alina asked her mum where daddy was, her mum got very cross so she didn't ask again. They had hardly any money, and the little girl no longer had new toys to play with. Instead she had to help her mother who took in other people's ironing to make ends meet.

Then one day, when Alina was fourteen, Mum brought home a new dad for her. Nico was not at all like her real dad and Alina didn't like him one bit. When he had been in the house for about six months he started to do very bad things to her when her mum was out. Alina was frightened and didn't dare tell anyone. Nico said that it was their little secret and that if she told anyone he would kill her. Alina didn't know what to do.

One day her mum asked her why she was always grumpy, so Alina took a deep breath and told her what Nico was doing. Mum was very angry and called her a liar and all sorts of other really bad names. She told her to go and never come back. She would not listen to her Alina's pleading, so all the girl could do was pack a few things in a bag and leave the house for good.

She travelled for many months across Europe. Sometimes she slept in barns, sometimes in bus or railway stations. She raided bins for food and begged for coins on street corners. Once she got a job cleaning up in a café, but the boss wanted her to get into his car with him after work. She did this once, and found out that he was as bad as Nico so she ran away again.

All this took a very long time, and Alina was tired of living on the streets. She wanted a proper home, with a fireplace and a cat just like she used to have when she was little. She had heard that if you went to England they would give you money, a place to live and a job. How she got to England is really another story, but I can tell you that she did eventually get there and she arrived in London two days before her sixteenth birthday at the end of November.

It wasn't at all like she'd been told. It was cold and dirty and no one even took the time to be horrid to her. She did get some money, but it wasn't enough to find anywhere to live and it was quickly gone on food and bus fares. Without anywhere to live Alina couldn't find a job and without a job she was worse off than she had been in all the other countries that she'd been through.

The people hurrying to and from the train station where she begged weren't usually downright rude. Some were, they directly commented on her dirty face, her scruffy clothes even her attempts to speak English. But mostly they ignored her, rushed past her as if she simply wasn't there and avoided any eye contact that might have breached some of her loneliness.

The police could be a problem. Mostly they just ignored her, but sometimes they moved her on from a sheltered doorway just as she had got comfortable. One young policeman once gave her some money for a hot drink and on one occasion another suggested she should find a hostel, but mostly they left her alone.

As Christmas approached the crowds increased and seemed to get even more frantic. Alina didn't even look at the food in all the shop windows, she ignored the bulging bags everyone was carrying and refused to think about the warm and loving Christmases of her long lost childhood.

Then she got a job.

A man called Mr Smith gave her a suitcase full of brightly coloured scarves. If she could sell them he would pay her for each item sold. He made it quite clear that she would have to pay for any that got lost or stolen. He would send his friend Duwayne round every day to collect the money.

But no one was interested in her wares; no one listened to her pleas to 'Buy my beautiful scarves.' One woman even shouted at her: 'Go away scarf girl.' The police took more interest in her now; they kept moving her on and demanding to see her licence. Duwayne changed from being friendly to threatening as every day she told him 'No scarves sold.'

As another hopeless day drew to a close Alina realised that nothing would change. Sadly she took her bag of scarves into the yard behind a closed-down shop. There she made a little house out of cardboard boxes and a few empty crates. She tried to eat a piece of bread she had found, but couldn't. So she spread some of the scarves on the concrete and wrapped the others around her. As the rest of London celebrated Christmas she drifted off to sleep.

Then a miracle happened.

As she lay there sick, tired and cold her father came to her. He picked her up and carried her gently back to her home. In front of the fire her mother sat roasting chestnuts, the cat asleep at her feet. There was no sign of Nico, just a table covered with delicious food. She smiled happily. Safe at last.

And that's how the security guard found her on

Boxing Day, wrapped in gaudy cloths, her head on a bag of rubbish, and a smile of peace and serenity on her cold, stiff face.

About the Author
Penny Rogers writes mainly short stories and flash fiction. You can find out more about her at www.pennyrogers.wordpress.co.uk

Scream

Roger Noons

A glass of Glogg (spiced red wine)

'Come on Edward, time for your birthday drink.'
'You go ahead, I'll see you in the pub.'
I stared across the fjord. I can't miss this sunset, blood and tongues of flame, it's amazing. I scribbled in my book, made some rough marks, hoped I would be able to read my notes.

I was in the studio within minutes and grabbed pastels, there already being a card on the easel. I slashed pigment onto the board. Stood back, consulted my notes and added more marks.

Standing back a second time, I knew I'd captured something special, but would it sell?

About the Author
Roger Noons is one of Cafélit's most prolific contributors with stories also selected for *Best of CaféLit 3* and *Best of CaféLit 4*. While the advent door was opened late he chose this for December 12th in honour of Edvard Munch's birthday.

Wake up Call
Linda Flynn

Golden Dream (a cocktail)

Catch a cliché full of illusory situations as we open the curtains to the pantomime of life…

Once upon a time, in a land far away, there was a beautiful princess, who was as fair as fair can (unnaturally) be. She was as good as she was beautiful, which in case you were wondering, was very good indeed.

Her only problem was that she required an excessive amount of beauty sleep, one hundred years to be precise.

So, when the handsome prince in tight fitting breeches found her, she was enjoying a little shut eye.

One sight of her completely took his breath away. (To tell the truth he was also a tad breathless on account of having to hack his way through the undergrowth surrounding the castle, as a good gardener could not be found for love or money.) Which was almost as bad as wading through her massive shoe collection, in fact he nearly got himself impaled on one of her ruby slippers. But then a girl can never have too many pairs of shoes.

Anyway, to cut to the chase, the prince kissed

her ruby red, perfect Cupid's bow lips. When she could get a word in edgeways, the princess opened her big brown Bambi eyes and said: 'My Prince!' Which was perhaps a bit presumptuous and premature.

Notwithstanding, they married in haste in an intimate ceremony, with just a thousand or two honoured guests, some of whom they knew.

Certainly the blushing bride looked radiant at the side of her perfect prince, as she anticipated a life of wedded bliss in the happily ever after.

True, she had a problem or two with her mother-in-law, who would put a hard pea under the mattress of her bed and who gave her a glass slipper as a bit of a joke. She wasn't sure about all that stuff about talking to her reflection in the mirror either.

Even the prince appeared to have picked up one or two bad habits on the way. He certainly owned some beautiful things, but in her opinion he spent far too much time frantically rubbing on his magic lamp.

Of course he was entitled to own his ugly duckling and his share of furry friends, after all every dog must have his day; it was just that pushy little Puss in Boots that she couldn't stand.

Over time she began to realise that he wasn't everyone's cup of tea, particularly hers, but that there was no point in crying over spilt milk.

Nor could she really understand why the prince would insist upon climbing up her long flowing hair to reach their tower room, when there was a perfectly good spiral staircase.

On reaching the summit he would scratch his head and mutter 'I'm sure I came in here for something.'

It was at that point that she realised that the perfect prince she had married had turned into a flipping frog.

The best that she could hope for was to wake up and discover that it had all been just a dream.

About the Author
Linda Flynn has had two humorous novels published: *Hate at First Bite* for 7-9 year olds and *My Dad's a Drag*, for teenagers. Both won Best First Chapter in The Writers' Billboard competition.

She has six educational books with the Heinemann Fiction Project. In addition she has written for a number of newspapers and magazines, including theatre reviews and several articles on dogs.

Her short stories with Bridge House include: two adult stories, *To Take Flight*, in the *Going Places* anthology and *I knew it in the Bath* in *Something Hidden*, as well as *The Wild Ones*, for teenagers in *Devils, Demons and Werewolves*. Two children's short stories: *The Secret Messenger* and *Timid Tim* were included in *Hippo-Dee-Doo-Dah*.

On 15th November 2015, Linda's latest short story, *Snowdrop* was published in the Bridge House Christmas anthology, *Snowflakes*.

Linda also works as a Head of English and PR at a school in Middlesex. Her interests include swimming, reading, walking her rescue dogs and far too much time spent daydreaming.

An Alternative Nativity

Laura van Weegen

*An iced black guillermo
(an espresso over a couple slices of lime)*

6 months to 0 AD

@The1TheOnlyBigG
Finally I've 'done' the deed. I'm going to be a daddy. :o>
Retweets: 3 Favourites: 1

Day before 0 AD

@JoeDaCarpenter @The1TheOnlyBigG The "virgin" mother is about to pop & I've got to pay the bleeding tax. #GiveUsASubMate #RipOffJudea
Retweets: 2,678 Favourites: 467

Day before 0 AD

@MaryDollBC In a stable having a baby!!! Scared but can't change my mind now. LOL. Hope @The1TheOnlyBigG can make it. ;)
Retweets: 897 Favourites: 936

Day before 0 AD

@The1TheOnlyBigG
Alas no but remember @JoeDaCarpenter

#GoodGuy #HesAKeeper
Retweets: 639 Favourites: 437

0 AD

@JoeDaCarpenter Proud of ya @MaryDollBC & good news is he has all his essentials #JesusAFutureSuperStar
Retweets: 3,897 Favourites: 1,523

0 AD + 1

@MaryDollBC One proud mama but going to have to change my Twitter account to @MaryDollAD. #1stWorldProblem. ;D
Retweets: 32,945 Favourites: 76,113

0 AD

@ImABaadBoy Work slow but anyone else seen... #NewStarInSky. Sod the sheep tonight I off to check this out. Boom! Who's coming?
Retweets: 21,765 Favourites: 13,439

0 AD

@PeteTheFollower @ImABaadBoy Where you at, want to join the fun??
Retweets: 105 Favourites: 27

0 AD

@ImABaadBoy @PeteTheFollower Bethlehem. Get here quick, it's all about to kick off!!!
Retweets: 105,694 Favourites: 78,682

0 AD

@The3Hipsters Woah #NewStarInSky #JesusAFutureSuperStar - Do u see a link? We do. #Booyashaka!!! Going to buy cool stuff for the wee man!
Retweets: 345,678 Favourites: 245,781

0 AD

@JoeDaCarpenter #WasntExpectingThat @The3Hipsters @TheBaadBoy Thanx for gifts & stuff @MaryDollBC is delighted.
Retweets: 655,129 Favourites: 489,781

0 AD + 1

@The3Hipsters #JesusAFutureSuperStar Watch out for his tour people, he's going to be huge. #YouHeardItHereFirst
Retweets: 818,336 Favourites: 1,027,472

0 AD + 1

@JoeDaCarpenter

Knackered.com but need to get the boy on the road #TheTourStartsNow #JesusAFutureSuperStar, first stop Egypt.
Retweets: 2,489,557 Favourites: 1,936,651

About the Author
Laura likes playing with new forms of language and is partial to a bit of #Flash. #JustSaying ;)

Santaphobia
Susan A. Eames

Mango Smoothie

Chloe hated Christmas. She hated the hype. She hated the premature TV commercials. She hated the shops with their unimaginative, repetitive decorations. She hated the annual regurgitation of Christmas music playing on a monotonous loop. Most of all, she hated Father Christmas.

As a child, she had been traumatised by the large man dressed in red with his big white beard. She had been taken to see Santa in his grotto and forced to sit in his capacious lap. When two hairy hands enfolded her and stroked her hair like a creepy murderer soothing his victim, she froze. But when she smelt his sour breath as he chanted 'Ho ho ho,' she screamed in panic until her mother rescued her from his clutches.

When she learned that this terrifying man was going to actually come down the chimney into her own home on Christmas Eve she refused to sleep alone. So Chloe's despairing parents told her the truth about the myth of Father Christmas at the tender age of four and a half.

Chloe never lost her fear of creepy Santa in his grotto and even into adulthood her loathing had developed into a full blown irrational, but very real, phobia.

Of course, it wasn't difficult to avoid these pseudo-Santas when she grew up. She solved the problem by holidaying every Christmas in countries that had no such traditions.

This year she chose Fiji, safe in the knowledge that a holiday on a South Pacific island was about as far removed from Santa with his sledge and snow-dusted reindeer as one could imagine. But Chloe had failed to do her research and didn't know that Christian missionaries had transformed the Cannibal Isles in the nineteenth century.

She walked along the dusty main street in a shocked daze. Upbeat versions of traditional Carols blared. Tatty fake Christmas trees and limp tinsel adorned the shops. She turned a corner and was confronted by the most extraordinary Santa in his grotto that she'd ever seen. Her instinct to flee was overshadowed by curiosity as she stared at the apparition. This was an interpretation of Santa in his grotto like no other.

The grotto was a bower fashioned from coconut palm fronds, decorated with red and pink hibiscus flowers and sweet scented frangipani. Like many Fijian men, Santa was absolutely gorgeous. Built like your archetypal rugby player, muscles bulged under his red t-shirt and shorts. No faux white beard or big belly for this Santa. He wore the traditional red hat, but with the addition of red hibiscus flowers tucked behind his ears.

Apart from his good looks, perhaps the most arresting difference was his cool dude sunglasses.

He seemed to be enjoying himself hugely – laughing and beckoning to the children who willingly went to him, shouldering each other in their eagerness to sit on his lap.

For the first time in her life, Chloe wanted to sit on Santa's lap too.

About the Author
Susan A. Eames left England over twenty-five years ago to explore the world and dive its oceans. She has had travel articles and short fiction published on three continents. After several fascinating years living in Fiji she has relocated to West Cork in Ireland.

Susan blogs at:
http://susan-a-eamestravelfictionandphotos.blogspot.ie

The Chimes At Midnight
Paula R C Readman

Chilli Chocolate and Red Wine

I cross the wide expanse of the lawn at the front of Crowhurst Hall; a journey I've made many times before. However, this time it feels different.

High above me the hunter's moon casts its lengthy shadows as the first flurries of the season snowfall, swirling around me, whipped up by the bitter wind. Tugging at the fabric of my skirt it seems to sweep me up and carries me over the threshold of my home.

In the cold hallway I stand dressed in what was once my finery before the old long-case clock, studying its delicate, ornate hands. In the past, as a child, I found them fascinating too, but then they marked the passing of a happier time. Now as I watch the seconds tick away, I wait for its hourly chime, but they do not come.

Evoking some half-remembered remark, I recall the past and the present like the sweeping hands of a clock run together. Yet, it seems like only yesterday when I heard it ring out its melancholy chimes to mark my passing. They resonated around my ice-cold body before the soil fell clattering upon my coffin lid as the mourners left me beneath the frosty ground.

Now the only sound I hear is the ticking of the clock as I wonder what has disturbed the tranquillity of my eternal slumber.

I know I cannot remain for long within these walls for I'm no longer welcome. He who robbed me of everything I held so dear would be outraged to know I've returned once more.

My faded, black taffeta skirt rustles on the stone tiled floors as I move aimlessly around. For a moment I linger in the library as wisps of tenebrous memories comes flooding back.

Suddenly I'm aware of some unfinished business, which may account for my homecoming. Climbing the marble staircase I pause; resting my hand lightly on its carved banister. Glancing up I see the gentle smiling faces of my beloved parents whom, with vacant, painted eyes stare back at me.

As I reminisce about their untimely passing, something cold creeps across the back of my bony neck and shoulders making me shudder. I brush my fingertips across my icy cheek longing to feel unshed tears washing my face with warmth as I cry for what was once mine.

I enter my old dressing room and find that the chilling night air fills it with dampness. Prior to my death my servant, Annie, would've made sure a welcoming fire filled it with warmth and light, but now it's as welcoming as a cold, empty grave.

In the past, I would've sat before the large ornate mirror, with its exquisite carvings of cherubs, love hearts, and doves, combing my glossy, golden tresses while dreaming of my darling Henry's return from London.

I recall too how my heart leapt with pleasure on hearing the sound of his carriage on the cobbles outside my window, knowing soon in his embrace I would hear his sweet, whispered words of love.

Now seated before it all I see is bone-dry, cadaverous skin stretching across my emaciated face as I brush dirt and worms from all that remain of my hair.

Has time passed me by so quickly that I'm nothing, but bones?

The sound of the door catch lifting brings me out of my reverie and I dissolve into the shadows as a young girl, just ripening into womanhood glides into the room. Crossing the pool of moonlight she heads in my direction.

Her beauty astounds me.

With raven-black hair, she's clothed only in a long, white nightgown, her bare feet blue with cold. She moves around the room with exaggerated movements while opening and closing the drawers and cupboard doors. In her dream-like state, she seems to be searching for something.

'How could he betray me so?' she mutters.

Stepping out of the shadows, I whisper 'Hello, young beauty, I wonder, did I disturb your slumber?'

Though her tear-stained eyes are unblinking, something flickers across her forlorn face makes me realise that, unlike me, death has no claim on her, but something disturbs the noctambulist's sleep.

I follow her, but she shows no signs that she's conscious of me.

Please, do not be afraid. I mean you no harm. What disturbs your sleep?' I ask.

She turns, her golden eyes dart back and forth as though seeking out a sound.

Aah, she does not see me, but hears me.

She lifts her left hand to brush a strand of her raven hair from her lips when something shimmers in the moonlight.

'What's this you're wearing?' I raise my bony, dust-dry hand before her face so she can see what hangs on my fleshless finger. 'It's a ring? So he's wed another, making us three?' I say as my heart breaks, knowing I've failed again.

Bewilderment settles on her face as her eyes begin to dilate, I realise then she sees me as a dream. Her soft voice carries neither weight nor sound, like a child's sleeping breath, she asks: 'Who are you?'

'I'm Eleanor,' I say 'I'm back from whence I slept so peacefully to warn you. Though I've failed another I once tried to save. Fate was so cruel.'

Her young brow creases as she stares right through me, then, as if she's suddenly aware that I'm standing there.

She steps back. Her hand flies to her mouth to stifle a cry. With trembling lips, she utters 'Incubus, Succubus, be gone!'

In contempt, I shake my shrunken head as dirt, worms, and hair falls from me scattering around my bony feet.

'I am neither. You may have youth and beauty on your side, but your days are numbered. As you see me standing before you, so you shall be one day. For there's no escaping from the hands of time. I wish only to see you grow old and not die before time has lined your face.'

Suddenly the sound of the tolling clock echoes with the passing of another hour.

'At last,' I cry, holding out my fleshless arms as the mournful chimes resound through the sleeping house, and the ravages of time are undone.

I stand clothed once more, flesh upon flesh, muscle, and sinew. Time restores my golden blonde tresses, but I cannot linger. Vanity is a weakness for living as time isn't mine.

She too wakes into half-sleep and whispers 'You're Lady Eleanor. I've seen your portrait, and your tomb in the cemetery. Five years have passed since you were murdered by an unknown intruder while your husband was away.'

'What tale is this? Come; let me show you the truth, for it too will be your fate, if you aren't careful.'

'Not the truth!' with a shudder, she hurries to her bedroom.

I follow her in fear she'll wake him.

In my haste I step into her bedroom. I'm surprised to find how little has changed. All that we selected together for our love nest he now shares with another.

Wiping her tears, the noctambulist stares down at her sleeping husband.

'Fear not, he sleeps,' say I.

She glances in my direction, her lower lip trembles as she whispers: 'When I see him sleeping so peacefully, my heart is full of love. The way the curls of his black hair fall lightly on his ruddy cheek. See how his lips part as he breathes gently. See the line of his jaw, so strong. How could you not fall for such a man?'

I laugh, 'Sweet nightwalker, if you heart is full of so much love for this sleeping man, then what makes you roam alone while he sleeps so serenely?'

A questioning look flickers across her innocent face. 'Should I not fear you, Lady Eleanor, for am I not talking in my disturbed sleep with a ghost?'

'I'm not here to do you harm. The living should not fear us who've passed over. We can do you no injury, sweet child. There's one who is living that you need to fear far more.'

'How can I trust you, you who have no right to be here?'

'Let me join you in your nocturnal amble through my home. For I was a child here...'

'This much I know,' say she.

'What troubles you so?'

She gestures to the room, 'There was another who called this house her home, but unlike you, she's not a ghost.'

'Come; let's go where we can talk more freely.'

As the noctambulist leaves, her husband rolls over. I feel the darkness within the room rearrange itself as I wait for him to awake so I can peer into his dark, soulless green eyes once more, but he sleeps on.

In the hallway, apart from the steady ticking of the clock, the only other sound is that of the noctambulist's bare feet on the stone floor as we enter the library.

As though she's fully awake, she crosses to the fireplace and adds another log to the dying embers. With a crackle, the fresh dry wood ignites throwing its warmth and light around the room, but although its heat cannot warm my dry bones, I still shudder as the shadows of my past gathered in every corner waiting for me to tell my tale of betrayal.

'Please can you tell me about the other woman?' I ask, though I fear the worst. For I had visited her on such a night, at least three years ago, to warn her the best I could that death would be at her door. Unlike this noctambulist, the second wife did not have a strong constitution.

On that night before the clock struck the hour to restore me, I had stepped out of the shadows too early and she had gazed upon my worm eaten face. Her pitiful screams woke what was left of her household.

Standing at the French windows, the sleepwalker has her back to me, staring at the moon through the lightly falling snow.

She turns and with a heavy sigh saying, 'My husband has no right to marry me when he has a wife who lives in a mental asylum. I uncovered Lady Helen's journal in the library and read about her fear of destitution. Her fears slowly descended her into madness. Unlike me, she was not strong, when Henry left her alone for days to travel to London. She feared he wouldn't return. All too soon, the servants deserted her. With no money to pay them their wages, she roamed the icy corridors alone.

'Now you appeared, haunting me in my dreams... Oh, why do I doubt the man I love so true?'

'Do you not believe her?' I ask, on hearing the

hesitation in her voice. 'Once I was like you believing every word he uttered. Now I am, but a ghost belonging to the borderland. Like Lady Helen and you, he deceived me too. Not for love he married me, but my father's money. The day he drove the knife into my beating heart, he took pleasure in telling me so.'

'Were you not killed by an unknown hand?' she asks, puzzlement lining her clear complexion.

'No. The hand that took my life was none other than that of my husband, Henry. In this very room, he drove in his knife taking such delight in telling me how he'd taken my parents' lives too, by having their carriage driven off the road. He'd discovered that my father had made inquiries in London's high society, finding out that among the gambling set Henry was notorious for being in debt.

With my dying breath, I cursed him. That's why I'm not free to sleep for eternity, until he has paid his debts in full to me.'

'Oh, it's all true,' she sobs, 'he married me for my money too. While he has been away, I uncovered his secrets here in the library. I found Lady Helen's journal and a bloodied knife. I wanted so much to know the truth,' Noctambulist whispers with a heavy-heart.

She crosses to a shelf. Half-hidden in shadows, pulls out a jewelled handled knife, and lays it before me.

'It's the knife,' I utter, 'with which he took my life.'

Suddenly, the library door bursts open and Henry steps in. On seeing the noctambulist sitting alone, he booms 'Oh, I do declare, my new wife betrays me not with another, but I feel madness fills the air yet again.' Laughing, he continued, 'Am I so cursed to find that another I took to be my bride suffering from lunacy too.'

I whisper to the noctambulist, 'Dear lady, pray take your leave. The time has come to set us free. Take Lady Helen's journal and keep it safe. Sleep deeply now until daybreaks.'

Picking up the book, the noctambulist turns her back on Henry, and takes her leave without a word.

He goes to follow, but the door slams shut. Watching in horror, he sees the key spin in the lock and vanishes.

'What trickery is this?' he cries in surprise.

Then out of the shadows, I appear still beautiful in a dark unnatural way, as I was on the day he took my life.

'None that I can see, my Lord, but revenge for those you've betrayed with your lies.' Laughing, I lift the knife, 'An eye for an eye.'

His eyes widen with fear as the cold of the grave radiates from me. His face pales as he raises his trembling hands as if to protect himself.

'This cannot be; you're a ghost that I should not

see. Dear God, help me and send this devil back to the ground where she should be.'

The French windows burst open as the fire goes out. Shadows draw around him with a sudden lurch; he drops to the ground. Protruding from his chest, the bejewelled knife immersed in his cold, black heart.

I stand over him as his confused spirit begins to rise.

Staring down at his dying self, he whispers 'What have you done to me?'

Time to pay for your sins. Now come follow me,' I turn towards the open doors.

You cannot do this to me! I'm still breathing and can be saved,' he screams. With a wave of my hand, he has no choice and reluctantly trails after me.

We cross the lawn to the cemetery. In the freshly fallen snow, only his footprints will be seen by everyone when the new day breaks.

In the distance, I hear the old hall clock ring out its melancholy chimes for the passing of the hour as the old day becomes the new. I sink into my grave, dragging with me what remained of Henry's conscious self, down to lay at my side.

Suddenly aware of his surroundings, Henry turns to face me, just as the worms slither back into my eye sockets, nostrils, mouth, and hair as time takes back what it had restored to me. His scream fills our narrow space.

'Oh, such joys at last to have you here beside me in this cold ground, dearest Henry. Did you think you could escape our wedding vows? Let no man put asunder not even death could keep us part.'

As I slip peacefully into eternal sleep with my husband at my side, the tombstone above our head now tells the truth; 'An unknown intruder murdered us who lie beneath this cold, cold ground.'

About the Author
Paula R C Readman has won two short story competitions one of which was the Harrogate Crime Writing competition, when Mark Billingham picked her story as the overall winner. She has also been published by English Heritage, Parthian Books and Bridge House in their anthologies. To find out more about her writing: paulareadman1.wordpress.com

Christmas on the High Street
Dawn Knox

Unsweetened cranberry juice – seasonal but bitter and harsh

Like a rock in a river, he stood, while shoppers flowed around him, their faces resolute and haunted. No one acknowledged him. Their eyes darted this way and that, as they sought the quickest route into each shop.

Well, there was so much to do on Christmas Eve.

A young girl stopped in front of him and looked up silently, with questioning eyes, before her mother seized her hand and dragged her back into the crowd.

They'd celebrate his birthday tomorrow or that's what they would claim to be doing. In reality, they didn't want to know him at all.

About the Author
Dawn Knox is married with one son and has been writing for several years. She has had a YA ebook published, entitled *Daffodil and the Thin Place* and has written a script for a play to commemorate World War One, which has been performed in her home town and in Germany. Dawn enjoys a writing challenge and has had stories published in various anthologies, including horror and speculative fiction, as well as romances in several women's magazines.

Telling The Time
Allison Symes

Cappuccino

I inherited the beautiful grandfather clock, aptly, from my grandfather. He swore it kept better time than Big Ben. I tried telling him that was the name of the bell but he was having none of it.

Much as I miss my grandfather, part of me is glad he isn't around to see his wonderful clock has gone horribly wrong. It has not been the same since that mouse got into the workings. Instead of chiming the hour, the bloody thing squeaks now.

On the plus side, I always know when it is 1 o'clock.

About the Author
Allison Symes is published by CaféLit, Bridge House Publishing, Alfie Dog Fiction, Scriggler.com and Shortbread Short Stories. She is a member of the Society of Authors and Association of Christian Writers. Her website is www.fairytaleswithbite.weebly.com and blogs for Chandler's Ford Today – http://chandlersfordtoday.co.uk/author/allison-symes/

Night Shift
B. Lieve

Cold Milk

Small fingers pressed lightly to glass, tracing circles in the mist. Listening for the soft magical tinkle of sound that says he's come. They laughed at her in school. *You don't really still believe he will, do you?*

She listens for the silent tramp of snowy boots, the creak of the armchair, the soft pad of footsteps on the stairs, imagines mince pie crumbs in his beard. He must come, he promised.

As she turns she hears it; a soft magical tinkle of sound. A key in the door. Her mum's voice. *Dad?* This year he did make it home.

About The Author
If you believe it, he will come.

On Repeat
James Phillips

A cup of cold, stewed tea

Harry sips his tea and glares at a glittering purple reindeer, which sits on a shelf above the seat opposite his. It is one of many small and glittery decorations scattered around Maggie's Diner. Christmas songs are playing through the café's speakers; not loud enough to prevent conversation, but still obtrusive and annoying. A new song comes on the sound system, lots of sleigh bells chiming and jingling. He's sure that he must have heard it three times already this morning. Harry thinks that the problem with Christmas songs is that there aren't enough of them and so they all come round again and again, on repeat, day after day. It's the same for the whole of December and it happens every year. It occurs to him that a good way to make his fortune is to write a new Christmas song every day. If he starts on the first of January and publishes the whole lot on the thirtieth of November, that will give him three hundred and thirty three songs. If each one averages three minutes and thirty seconds; Harry wrestles with the mental arithmetic, he's faced with an endless series of threes and keeps losing count. He takes his notebook and the stub end of a pencil out of his pocket and writes the sum down, showing his workings just like Mrs Lettuce insisted. He starts to wonder if Mrs Lettuce is really the name of his old teacher, but then the numbers in his notebook catch his eye and bring him back to Christmas song writing. Three hundred and thirty three, he writes, multiplied by three, is nine hundred and ninety nine; add in the three hundred and three extra sets of thirty seconds and it comes to one thousand four hundred and forty eight minutes and thirty seconds.

Harry looks at this number and decides that it's a good number. He is on the verge of going as far as to call it a very good number when he realises that it doesn't mean very much as it is. He needs to convert minutes into hours. Harry feels an initial edge of panic grip him. He's going to have to divide by a number that is greater than nine. His long division has never been very strong and the spectre of Mrs Lettuce is so real that he can smell the lily of the valley. He is about to give up on the whole thing when he realises that, instead of sixty, he can divide by six and just move a decimal point afterwards and this makes him much happier. The memory of Mrs Lettuce fades and he starts to do the division. Half way through the sum, he stops when he realises that the answer comes to a bit more than two hundred and forty. He moves the decimal point and gets twenty four hours; a whole day. He's done it!

Harry imagines himself meeting the Queen to receive his OBE and being received at Number Ten. He will be hailed as the man who saved Christmas. Everyone will be so much happier when no song has to be played more than once per day in the festive season.

It is a lovely image and Harry smiles as he pours himself a cup of cold, stewed tea from the white china pot he's been nursing for hours. The tea doesn't pour very well, dribbling into his saucer and onto the table top, where it mingles with the crumbs of a sandwich from earlier on.

What the world needs, is a universal spout design for teapots so that they all pour properly.

He imagines himself designing the perfect spout, installing a potter's wheel and a kiln in his shed. Well, okay, getting a shed, erecting it and then installing them. He'll have to attend pottery classes of course, but he has no doubt that he will show natural aptitude. How could it be otherwise when he is being driven by his vision of a perfectly poured cup of tea?

Maggie appears at his table and replaces the old pot with a new one.

'There you are, Harry love,' she says, 'that one must be stewed and gone cold by now.'

She turns and returns to behind the counter and Harry watches her go.

A new song comes on the sound system, lots of

sleigh bells chiming and jingling. He's sure that he must have heard it three times already this morning. Harry thinks that the problem with Christmas songs is that there aren't enough of them and so they all come round again and again, on repeat, day after day. It's the same for the whole of December and it happens every year.

About the Author
James Phillips is a house husband from Bangor, North Wales. He spends his days writing, drinking tea and avoiding housework and his evenings playing and promoting live music. His blog is at
https://jamespmphillips.wordpress.com/

Index Of Drinks

A caffeine shot	47
A cup of cold, stewed tea	108
A glass of absinthe	45
A glass of dandelion and burdock	33
A glass of Glogg (spiced red wine)	81
A glass of milk and a cookie	38
A large mug of hot chocolate	48
A mug of hot sweet tea	11
An iced black guillermo (an espresso over a couple slices of lime)	86
Aqua Libra	18
Black Coffee	55
Black coffee: keep it coming	46
Bucks Fizz	60
Campari soda	34
Cappuccino	106
Chilli Chocolate and Red Wine	93
Cold Milk	107
Cup of hot sweet Rooibos Tea	35
G and T	40
Glass of chilled Singha Beer	73
Golden Dream (a cocktail)	82
(Hot chocolate) with sprinkles?	20
J.W. Lees bitter	28
Mango Smoothie	90
Pepsi	25
Shoo-Fly Punch	54
Tap Water	76
Tea turned cold on a window ledge	49
Tea; gone cold	13
The Goldeneye – Smooth cocktail made from rum and pineapple juice. Served with a wedge of pineapple.	10
Unsweetened cranberry juice – seasonal but bitter and harsh	105

Writing For CaféLit

Have you got a story in you? Do you think it would suit CaféLit?

We're looking for thought-provoking and entertaining stories, though ones which might be a tad different from what you normally read in a woman's magazine. They should be the sort of length that would make easy reading whilst you drink a cup of coffee, even if you linger a while, but without you needing to rent a table.

So, perhaps, no more than 3000 words. Shorter stories and flash fiction are naturally very welcome.

We'll read your story. If we like it, we'll let you know and if we don't like it we'll let you know – within a month. We will work on editing with you.

Each year we'll publish a volume of the best stories. If you are in the volume you will have a share of the profits.

Our editing process will also include some work on your bio to maximise its effect.

We also ask you assign your story the name of a drink. Something light and frothy might be a hot chocolate. A dark piece of flash fiction could be an espresso. Something good for the soul would be a mint tea.

Full submission details can be found at www.cafelit.co.uk/page1.html.

Also By Chapeltown Books

The Best of CaféLit 4

Each story in this little volume is the right length and quality for enjoying as you sip the assigned drink in your favourite Creative Café. You need never feel alone again in a café. So what's the mood today? Espresso? Earl Grey tea? Hot chocolate with marshmallows? You'll find most drinks in our drinks index.

If you're reading the café's copy and you have your Kindle or iPhone with you, why not download the Kindle version? Or browse the CaféLit web site for more examples of CaféLit stories?

www.cafelit.co.uk

Order from http://chapeltownbooks.co.uk

ISBN: 978-1-910542-02-6 (paperback)
978-1-910542-03-3 (ebook)

Chapeltown Books